BIG DATA, BIG DUPE

BIG DATA, BIG DUPE

A little book
about a big bunch of nonsense

STEPHEN FEW

Analytics Press

Analytics Press

PO Box 4933
El Dorado Hills, CA 95762
SAN 253-5602
www.analyticspress.com
Email: info@analyticspress.com

© 2018 by Stephen C. Few

PUBLISHER: Bryan Pierce

COPY EDITOR: Nan Wishner
COMPOSITION: Bryan Pierce
COVER DESIGN: Nigel Holmes
PHOTOGRAPHY: Leanne Kruse
PRINTER AND BINDER: C&C Offset Printing Company

ISBN: 978-1-938377-10-5

This book was printed on acid-free paper in China.

10 9 8 7 6 5 4 3 2 1

Same as it ever was
Same as it ever was
Same as it ever was
Same as it ever was
Same as it ever was
Same as it ever was
Same as it ever was
Same as it ever was

"Once in a Lifetime," Talking Heads

ABOUT THE AUTHOR

Stephen Few has worked in IT for nearly 35 years and is best known for his contributions to the field of data visualization. Since founding his consultancy, Perceptual Edge, in 2003, Stephen has written four popular books on the subject:

> *Show Me the Numbers: Designing Tables and Graphs to Enlighten* (2nd edition)
>
> *Information Dashboard Design: Displaying Data for At-A-Glance Monitoring* (2nd edition)
>
> *Now You See It: Simple Visualization Techniques for Quantitative Analysis*
>
> *Signal: Understanding What Matters in a World of Noise*

Above all else, Stephen is a teacher. As such, he helps people learn how to use data more effectively to increase understanding and improve decision making.

When he isn't working, Stephen almost always has his head in a book pursuing a broad range of interests. He currently resides in Portland, Oregon, with his two dogs Enzo and Bella.

To the four teachers during my formative years who taught me that I was capable and had something worthwhile to say. Thank you Mrs. Land and Mr. Giardina of Woodlawn Avenue Elementary School in Bell, California and Mr. Aguilar and Mr. Hessler of Nimitz Junior High School in Huntington Park, California. Learning from you that my thoughts and words were important inspired me to find my voice and the courage to use it.

TABLE OF CONTENTS

A NOTE TO READERS

I hope this book has an extremely brief but productive lifespan. I would love for it to be a flash in the pan: an ignition of interest that quickly leads to a rise in awareness, resulting in the demise of Big Data, thus rendering the book obsolete. Unlike my other books, which were great labors of love, this book was thrust upon me by unbearable frustration. I began writing about the follies of Big Data back in 2012. Year after year, as Big Data continued to undermine people's hopes of gleaning value from data, I tried to chip away at it, always surprised that such nonsense would continue to reign over the minds of people who think of themselves as data literate. My frustration finally reached critical mass. Someone needed to write a book like *Big Data, Big Dupe*. I decided that it might as well be me.

This book draws extensively from articles that I've written during the past few years in the newsletter and blog of my consultancy, Perceptual Edge. I founded Perceptual Edge in 2003 to help people and organizations harvest value from data through courses, books, articles, and consulting services that focus on data visualization. By pulling content from several of my articles together, organizing it into a coherent argument, and expanding it to cover the territory more completely, I hope to have an impact that a smattering of separate articles appearing on a niche website could never manage.

A colleague who read the initial draft of this book suggested that I make it longer. He was concerned that a short book would not be taken seriously. I resisted his advice for two reasons. First, the book is a long as it needs to be. Second, I want this book to be read by the busy executives and managers who make the decisions that fund Big Data initiatives and purchases. Many of the people who actually work with data already know that Big Data is a ruse, but their bosses don't.

Although this isn't a labor of love, it is a labor of great purpose and necessity. We can do great things if we approach data intelligently. At this moment, Big Data is standing in the way.

INTRODUCTION – BIG DATA, BIG WHOOP

My parents named me Stephen. I've gone by the names Stephen and Steve my entire life. Imagine that you've known me for years, and I walk up to you one day and demand, "From now on I want you to call me Big Steve because I'm now a different person than I was before." You might decide to call me Big Steve as an act of courtesy, or perhaps out of concern that I've become a dangerous nut case, but you probably wouldn't believe that Big Steve was anything other than a narcissistic delusion. Now, imagine that I took this up a notch by demanding that you must not only call me Big Steve, but must also pay top dollar for my companionship. At this point, you'd begin to wonder what I'd been smoking and just how much my friendship was actually worth.

Around the year 2008, purveyors of data began to approach us and proclaim that we should begin to refer to some ill-defined new expression of data as Big Data. Big Data? Really? What has changed? In truth, nothing of substance or significance has changed. Everything that data is today it has been for a very long time. Everything that we fundamentally do to make sense of data today we've been doing for a very long time. So, what is Big Data? My aim in this book to pull back the curtain and reveal Big Data for what it is—or, more to the point, what it isn't.

During nearly 35 years of working in information technology (IT), I've encountered a lot of nonsense, but Big Data takes the cake. None of the silliness that has been dreamed up by high-tech marketing professionals has better illustrated Hans Christian Andersen's tale "The Emperor's New Clothes." Big Data has been strutting around in the buff for nearly a decade, and the world is still praising its illusory duds.

Every few years, IT vendors in the analytics space (business intelligence, data science, decision support, data visualization, statistics, etc.) unveil a new fashion line-up that is little more than the same old threadbare rags with a new name. They do this to drive growth to meet aggressive revenue goals, often to compensate for stalled sales due to poor performance and failed promises. Unfortunately, people and organizations can easily be fooled by impressive-sounding names and splashy campaigns. Big Data has perhaps been the most successful of these sleights of hand.

Don't mistake this critique of Big Data as a critique of data. Data, properly used, holds great promise. I've based my career on this understanding. But Big Data claims to be something more—something better—than data. It isn't. Big Data is an illusion that, if pursued, can, at a minimum, waste your time and money, and, at its worst, do great harm.

I love most things Italian. I've travelled to Italy many times and enjoy many things that that the country and its culture have to offer. I especially appreciate the passionate way in which many of my Italian friends express themselves. One of my favorite Italian exclamations is "Basta!" "Basta" means "enough," as in "ENOUGH of this!" In light of this, I propose "Basta, Big Data!" as a timely expression. We've definitely had enough of Big Data.

Why should we care about the false promise of Big Data? Most of the so-called thought leaders in the data industry don't seem to be concerned at all. They are riding high on Big Data's bandwagon, proclaiming the benefits as they pull in money hand over fist. I could stake out a prime spot of my own on that bandwagon, but I've never been tempted. This is because I care about the true potential of data for increasing understanding and informing high-quality decisions. In other words, I value the promises of data, and I know that these promises are hollow when they're tied to Big Data. What data promises can be acquired but only through time-proven, less-hyperbolic means.

But what about all of the great benefits that have been produced by Big Data? Some people and organizations have certainly derived value from data—success that they have attributed to Big Data. However, their efforts would have been just as successful had they been called by any other name. Nothing about Big Data enabled those successes.

Good people and organizations have been hoodwinked by Big Data. This includes many of those who have promoted it. They can't see that the emperor is naked, so they invest their time, money, energies, and hopes in illusory garments that leave them unprotected from the elements, shivering from hypothermia while they wrap themselves in expensive vaporware. They are no closer to the goal of deriving value from data than they were before they started down the Big Data highway. The goal of this book is to put us on a surer path to data's bounty. To do this, we must realize that the yellow brick road to Big Data ("the Great and Powerful") leads to a confused little sham of a wizard hiding behind a curtain.

A solid foundation for evidence-based understanding and decision making is not only worthwhile, it's increasingly necessary as our world becomes more complex and its challenges more threatening. No yellow brick road leads to this goal. There is a road—more of a path, actually—that will take us to this goal, but it isn't paved or frequently traveled. On this "road less travelled" we find conscientious people who have taken time to develop effective data-sensemaking skills. They use technologies to extend their reach, but they remain in charge, never trusting tools to do their thinking for them. This road hasn't changed much over the past few decades. Why is it seldom travelled? I think, in part, because we are drawn to easy, magical solutions over hard work. But the longer we pursue magical solutions instead of doing the work of thinking deeply and developing finely honed skills, the longer we will remain lost in growing mounds of data that we don't understand. It's time to move on. I've written this book to help us begin the journey.

Chapters 1 through 6 each reveal a different reason why Big Data is hollow, wasteful, and ultimately harmful. The epilogue is a call to action.

This book is an argument against Big Data and for the value of data. My aim is to convince you that my argument is valid and that

the consequences of ignoring it are dire. Nothing in these pages is
difficult to understand; read them thoughtfully, and decide for
yourself whether Big Data deserves derision or ongoing access to
your wallet.

CHAPTER 1 – BIG DATA, BIG CONFUSION

Big Data lacks meaning. It has never had a commonly accepted definition.

What is the origin of the term "Big Data" as it is used today? We actually don't know for certain, which is odd. The origins of recently coined terms, especially those related to technology, can usually be traced. The term "Big Data" emerged into popular consciousness around the year 2010. Known instances of the words "big" and "data" being used in combination date back to the late 1980s, but current uses of "Big Data" apparently weren't derived from them.

Historical Roots of the Term

In 1989, Erik Larson wrote an article for *Harper's Magazine* bemoaning junk email that included the following sentence: "The keepers of big data say they do it for the consumer's benefit." One of the next appearances of the term was in 1997 at the Institute for Electronics and Electronics Engineers (IEEE) 8th Conference on Visualization, in a paper by Michael Cox and David Ellsworth titled "Application-controlled demand paging for out-of-core visualization." The article began as follows:

> *Visualization provides an interesting challenge for computer systems: data sets are generally quite large, taxing the capacities of main memory, local disk, and even remote disk. We call this the problem of big data.* [1]

Two years later, at the 1999 IEEE Conference on Visualization, a panel convened titled "Automation or interaction: what's best for big data?" Two years after that, in 2001, Doug Laney, who worked for Meta Group at the time but now works for Gartner, published a research note titled "3D Data Management: Controlling Data Volume, Velocity, and Variety." The term Big Data did not appear in the report, but not long after the term emerged, Laney's "3Vs" (volume, velocity, and variety) became the characteristics that are most often attributed to Big Data.

The first time I ran across the term was in a 2005 email from the software company *Insightful*, the maker of S+, a derivative of the statistical analysis language R. The term appeared in the title of a course offered by the vendor: "Working with Big Data."

By 2008, the term had popped up often enough in academic circles to warrant a special issue of *Nature* magazine to "examine what big data sets mean for contemporary science." The concept of Big Data remained relatively obscure, however, even in academic circles, until 2010, when Kenneth Cukier, Data Editor of *The Economist*, wrote a special report in which he asserted:

> *...the world contains an unimaginably vast amount of digital information which is getting ever vaster ever more rapidly... The effect is being felt everywhere, from business to science, from governments to the arts. Scientists and computer engineers have coined a new term for the phenomenon: "big data."* [2]

Who, exactly, were the scientists and engineers who coined the term? Cukier didn't say. The timing of Cukier's report leads me to suspect that his use of the term in *The Economist* was noticed by some unidentified business or marketing professional who set in motion the most successful IT marketing campaign of recent years. Technology vendors routinely adopt one another's claims. The term "Big Data" spread like wildfire. Soon, every vendor in the data space was preaching the glories of Big Data.

Semantic Failure

In regard to expressing something meaningful, Big Data has been an utter failure. It has never managed to mean anything in particular. Rather, it tends to mean whatever people want it to mean or whatever serves their purposes in the moment. A term that means nothing in particular means nothing at all.

What exactly is Big Data? This question lacks a clear answer for the following reasons:

- There are almost as many definitions of Big Data as there are people with opinions. No commonly accepted definition exists.
- None of its many definitions describe anything about data and its use that is substantially different from what already existed or was being done in the past. As such, a new term isn't warranted.
- Most of the definitions are so vague or ambiguous that they cannot be used to determine, one way or the other, if a particular set of data or use of data qualifies as Big Data.

Allow me to illustrate the problem with a personal example. In 2014, I read an article on the website of *Scientific American* titled "Saving Big Data from Big Mouths" by Dr. Cesar A. Hidalgo. In the article, Hidalgo, who teaches in the Massachusetts Institute of Technology (MIT) Media Lab, challenged several other articles in prominent publications that dared to criticize the claims of Big Data. The fact that he characterized naysayers as "big mouths" clues us into his perspective on the matter. In reading his article, I noticed that Hidalgo at no point actually defined what he meant by Big Data, which concerned me. I expressed my concern by posting the following comments in response to his article on *Scientific American's* website:

> *I'm one of the naysayers in response to the claims of so-called Big Data. I'm concerned primarily with the hype that leads organizations to waste money chasing new technologies rather than developing the skills that are needed to glean value from data. One of the fundamental problems with Big Data is the fact that no two people define it in the same way, so it is difficult to discuss it intelligently. In this article, you praised the benefits of Big Data, but did not define it. What do you mean by Big Data? How is Big Data different from other data? When did data become big? Are the means of gleaning value from so-called Big Data different from the means of gleaning value from data in general?*

Hidalgo was kind enough to respond. Here's how he began.

> *As you probably know well, the term big data is used*
> *colloquially to refer mostly to digital traces of human*
> *activities. These include cell phone data, credit card records*
> *and social media activity. Big data is also used occasionally*
> *to refer to data generated by some scientific experiments (like*
> *CERN or genomic data), although this is not the most*
> *common use of the phrase so I will stick to the "digital traces*
> *of human activity" definition for now.*

Actually, I did not know well that the term Big Data was "used colloquially to refer mostly to digital traces of human activities." What Hidalgo assumed as the common definition of Big Data neither matched my experience nor that of most Big Data advocates. Instead, it matched his own experience with the term as an academic. I began my response to Hidalgo's comments with the following:

> *Your response regarding the definition of Big Data demon-*
> *strates the problem that I'm trying to expose: Big Data has*
> *not been defined in a manner that lends itself to intelligent*
> *discussion. Your definition does not at all represent a*
> *generally accepted definition of Big Data. It is possible that*
> *the naysayers with whom you disagree define Big Data*
> *differently than you do.*

Hidalgo's perception vividly illustrates the definitional quagmire in which Big Data resides. There are many definitions of Big Data, and they don't comfortably coexist. Many proponents of Big Data never actually define the term. This is true of many technology vendors, in particular, who benefit from leaving the term undefined.

Even the most popular book written about *Big Data to date, Big Data: A Revolution That Will Transform How We Live, Work, and Think* by Viktor Mayer-Schönberger and Kenneth Cukier, never actually defined the term. The authors did admit, however, that the term is ill-defined. Given this admission, I hoped that the authors would propose a definition of their own to reduce some of the confusion, but they never did. Instead, they described it in several disjointed ways. Here's one of their early descriptions:

> *The sciences like astronomy and genomics, which first experienced the explosion in the 2000s, coined the term "big data." The concept is now migrating to all areas of human endeavor.* [3]

So, from one perspective at least, Big Data is an "explosion" in scientific data. How else do the authors describe it? Big Data is "the ability of society to harness information in novel ways to produce useful insights or goods and services of significant value." [4] Anything else?

> *At its core, big data is about predictions. Though it is described as part of the branch of computer science called artificial intelligence, and more specifically, an area called machine learning, this characterization is misleading. Big data is not about trying to "teach" a computer to "think" like humans. Instead, it's about applying math to huge quantities of data in order to infer probabilities.* [5]

They go on. "But where most people have considered big data as a technological matter, focusing on the hardware or the software, we believe the emphasis needs to shift to what happens when the data speaks." [6] I'm not quite sure what this means. What happens when the data speaks? How does data speak? And more fundamentally, what separates Big Data from data of the past? Here's Mayer-Schönberger and Cukier's answer:

> *One way to think about the issue today—and the way we do in this book—is this: big data refers to things one can do at a large scale that cannot be done at a smaller one, to extract new insights or create new forms of value, in ways that change markets, organizations, the relationship between citizens and governments, and more.*
>
> *But this is just the start. The era of big data challenges the way we live and interact with the world. Most strikingly,*

society will need to shed some of its obsession for causality in exchange for simpler correlations: not knowing why but only what. This overturns centuries of established practices and challenges our most basic understanding of how to make decisions and comprehend reality. [7]

Hmmm. To "make decisions and comprehend reality," we no longer need to understand *why* things happen together (causation) but only *what* things happened together (correlation). When I read this, an eerie feeling crawled up my spine. The implications of this line of thinking are scary. I'll explain why in Chapter 5, "Big Data, Big Regression."

So, apparently Big Data consists of "things one can do at a large scale that cannot be done at a smaller one." What are these things, and how exactly do they change the way "we live and interact with the world?" This is never satisfactorily addressed in the book.

Where does the uniqueness of Big Data, as opposed to just plain old data, reside? "The real revolution is not in the machines that calculate data but in data itself and how we use it." [8] So, what's special about Big Data resides in the data itself. The authors go on to suggest that new reverence should be paid to data of the "Big Data" variety: "In the age of big data, all data will be regarded as valuable, in and of itself." [9]

For Mayer-Schönberger and Cukier, data in its new incarnation apparently deserves a standing ovation just for existing. Whether anything has fundamentally changed about data and its use to justify its new celebrity status, we'll consider in the next chapter. For our present purposes, we'll merely note that Big Data is a semantic mess.

In truth, the term Big Data continues to function today as it did when it first became popular—as a marketing campaign. As such, the term actually benefits from being unrooted to any particular meaning. Whatever it is that you think Big Data means, vendors can claim that they support it. Big Data is a source of fabricated need and endless confusion. Like email spam and those annoying ads that are always popping up in our Web browsers, Big Data refuses to go away.

Mismatched Ingredients of a Definitional Goulash

Let's get down to the specifics. The definitions of Big Data that I've encountered can be grouped into a few categories. Big Data means...

1. ...data sets that are extremely large (i.e., an exclusive emphasis on volume)
2. ...data from various sources and of various types, some of which are relatively new (i.e., an exclusive emphasis on variety)
3. ...data that is large in volume, derived from various sources, and produced and acquired at fast speeds (i.e., the three Vs of volume, velocity, and variety)
4. ...data that is extraordinarily complex
5. ...data that is processed using so-called advanced analytical methods
6. ...any data at all that is associated with a current fad

Let's consider the problems that are associated with definitions in each of these categories.

Data Sets That Are Extremely Large

Here we consider a few of the proposed definitions that feature size as the primary defining factor. According to the website of the statistical software company SAS: "Big data is a term that describes the large volume of data—both structured and unstructured—that inundates a business on a day-to-day basis." [10] This definition fails in several respects, not the least of which is its restriction to *business* data. The fundamental problem with definitions that focus primarily on the size of data sets as the defining factor, however, is their failure to specify how a large data set must be to qualify as Big Data rather than merely as data. What threshold must be crossed to move from data to Big Data?

Here's a definition that attempts to identify the threshold: "Big Data is a phrase used to mean a massive volume of both structured and unstructured data that is so large it is difficult to process using traditional database and software techniques." [11] Do you see the problem of defining the threshold in this manner? What are "traditional database and software techniques?" Also, must a data set always include both structured and unstructured data to qualify as Big Data, as this and the previous definition both suggest?

Source Note: Most of the following definitions of Big Data that appear in this chapter originally appeared in a September 3, 2014 article written by Jennifer Dutcher of the University of California, Berkeley School of Information, titled "What is Big Data?"

The following definition is slightly less vague: "Big data means data that cannot fit easily into a standard relational database." [12] Does this definition succeed in clarifying the threshold? It doesn't. In theory, there are no limits to the amount of data that can be stored in a relational database. Databases of all types have practical limits that usually stem from the hardware on which they reside. People have suggested other technology-based volume thresholds besides the capacity of relational databases, including data that cannot fit into an Excel spreadsheet. All of these definitions establish arbitrary limits. Some of these are based on arbitrary measures as well, such as the following: "Big data is data that even when efficiently compressed still contains 5-10 times more information (measured in entropy or predictive power, per unit of time) than what you are used to right now." [13] Apparently, if you are accustomed to 1,000 row Excel tables, a simple SQL Server database consisting of 5,000 to 10,000 rows qualifies as Big Data. Such definitions highlight the uselessness of arbitrary limits that are based on data volume.

Here's another definition that, with its list of "maybes," acknowledges Big Data's arbitrary threshold: "Big data is when...the standard, simple methods (maybe it's SQL, maybe it's k-means, maybe it's a single server with a cron job) break down on the size of the data set, causing time, effort, creativity, and money to be spent crafting a solution to the problem that leverages the data without simply sampling or tossing out records." [14]

Some definitions acknowledge the arbitrariness of the threshold but fail to recognize it as a definitional failure:

The term big data is really only useful if it describes a quantity of data that's so large that traditional approaches to data analysis are doomed to failure. That can mean that you're doing complex analytics on data that's too large to fit into memory or it can mean that you're dealing with a data storage system that doesn't offer the full functionality of a standard relational database. What's essential is that your old way of doing things doesn't apply anymore and can't just be scaled out. [15]

What good is a definition that is based on a subjective threshold in data volume? No good because it gives us no means to distinguish Big Data from other data.

The following definition refreshingly acknowledges that, when the criterion is data volume, what qualifies as Big Data not only varies from organization to organization but over time as well:

Big data is data that contains enough observations to demand unusual handling because of its sheer size, though what is unusual changes over time and varies from one discipline to another. Scientific computing is accustomed to pushing the envelope, constantly developing techniques to address relentless growth in dataset size, but many other disciplines are now just discovering the value—and hence the challenges—of working with data at the unwieldy end of the scale. [16]

Not only do these definitions identify Big Data in a manner that lacks objective thresholds, they also acknowledge (perhaps inadvertently) that Big Data has always been with us because data has always been increasing in ways that lead to processing challenges. In other words, Big Data is no different from data in the past. Big Data is just data.

There is a special breed of volume-based definition that advocates "Collect and store everything." Here is the most explicit and thorough definition of this sort that I've encountered:

The rising accessibility of platforms for the storage and analysis of large amounts of data (and the falling price per

TB of doing so) has made it possible for a wide variety of organizations to store nearly all data in their purview—every log line, customer interaction, and event—unaggregated and for a significant period of time. The associated ethos of "store everything now and ask questions later" to me more than anything else characterizes how the world of computational systems looks under the lens of modern "big data" systems. [17]

These "collect and store everything" definitions change the nature of the threshold between "data" and "Big Data" from a measure of volume to the assumption that we should collect everything at the lowest level of granularity whether useful or not, for we never know when it might become useful.

Definitions of this type are a hardware vendor's dream, but they are an organization's nightmare because the cost of unlimited storage extends well beyond the cost of hardware. The time and resources that are required to collect and store everything are enormous and rarely justified. Expert data sensemakers know that the vast majority of the data that exists in the world is noise and will always be noise. Don't line the pockets of hardware vendors with gold by buying into the ludicrous assumption that you should store every piece of data in case it might be useful one day.

Data from Various Sources and of Various Types

Some definitions of Big Data emphasize variety—the fact that it comes in various types and from various sources. Here's one of the clearest:

What's "big" in big data isn't necessarily the size of the databases, it's the big number of data sources we have, as digital sensors and behavior trackers migrate across the world. As we triangulate information in more ways, we will discover hitherto unknown patterns in nature and society— and pattern-making is the wellspring of new art, science, and commerce. [18]

Definitions that emphasize variety suffer from the same problems as those that emphasize volume: where is the threshold? How many data sources are needed to qualify data as Big Data? Definitions of Big Data never say.

Data That Exhibits High Volume, Velocity, and Variety

I'll use Gartner's definition to represent this category in honor of the fact that Doug Laney of Gartner was the first to identify the three Vs (volume, velocity, and variety) as the game changers that led to Big Data: "Big Data is high-volume, high-velocity and/or high-variety information assets that demand cost-effective, innovative forms of information processing that enable enhanced insight, decision making, and process automation." [19] Combining volume and variety, which we've already considered, then adding velocity—the speed at which data is generated and acquired—produces definitions that suffer from all of the problems that we've already encountered.

Another problem with 3V definitions is the fact that volume and velocity are largely redundant from a practical perspective. Saying that data is being produced faster than before is essentially no different than saying that data volumes are getting bigger at an increased rate. Both are just shorthand for "more." The one exception is those rare cases in which data must be analyzed immediately, in real time, such as for the stock trades that hedge funds make using analytical algorithms. However, we've learned that trusting these algorithms to make good decisions at lightening speeds without human interactions is a risky venture.

Data That Is Especially Complex

Some definitions focus on the complexity of data, such as the following:

> While the use of the term is quite nebulous and is often
> co-opted for other purposes, I've understood "big data" to be
> about analysis for data that's really messy or where you don't

know the right questions or queries to make—analysis that
can help you find patterns, anomalies, or new structures
amidst otherwise chaotic or complex data points. [20]

You can probably anticipate what I'm about to say about definitions of this sort: like several of the previous types of definitions we've looked at, definitions that focus on complexity lack a clear threshold. They don't explain what they mean by complexity, and they revolve around a quality that has always been true of data. How complex is complex enough, what constitutes complexity, and when was data *not* complex?

Data That Is Processed Using Advanced Analytical Methods

According to definitions in this category, there is nothing about the data itself that determines Big Data; instead it's the methods used to make sense of data that characterize it as Big Data. Here's an example: "The term 'big data' often refers simply to the use of predictive analytics, user behavior analytics, or certain other advanced data analytics methods that extract value from data." [21] Some of these definitions allow quite a bit of leeway regarding the nature of so-called advanced analytical methods while others are more specific, such as the following:

Big data is an umbrella term that means…the possibility of
doing extraordinary things using modern machine learning
techniques on digital data. Whether it is predicting illness,
the weather, the spread of infectious diseases, or what you
will buy next, it offers a world of possibilities for improving
people's lives. [22]

What analytical methods qualify as Big Data? Is it machine learning methods? The answer usually depends on the methods that the person who is defining Big Data happens to use or sell.

A few of the definitions in this category have emphasized advanced skills rather than technologies, such as the following:

As computational efficiency continues to increase, "big data" will be less about the actual size of a particular dataset and more about the specific expertise needed to process it. With that in mind, "big data" will ultimately describe any dataset large enough to necessitate high-level programming skill and statistically defensible methodologies in order to transform the data asset into something of value. [23]

These definitions do little to help us distinguish "analytical skills" from the "advanced analytical skills" that supposedly change our use of data in some fundamental and substantial way. Does "high-level programming skill" really set data analysis today apart from data analysis in the past? It doesn't. Ever since computers became readily available for data analysis, skilled analysts have developed programming skills to do their work because these skills have always been necessary to deal with the realities of messy data and to provide the flexibility needed to address unique analytical challenges. Does the need for "statistically defensible methodologies" represent a departure from the past? Of course not.

Any Data at All That Is Associated with a Current Fad

Some definitions of Big Data apply the term to anything regarding data that is trending. Here's an example: "I see big data as storytelling—whether it is through information graphics or other visual aids that explain it in a way that allows others to understand across sectors." [24] This tendency was directly acknowledged by Ryan Swanstrom: "Now big data has become a buzzword to mean anything related to data analytics or visualization." [25]

This is what happens with fuzzy definitions. They can be easily manipulated to mean anything you wish. As such, they are meaningless and useless.

The definitional messiness and thus uselessness of the term "Big Data" is far from unique. Many IT terms exhibit these dysfunctional traits. I've worked in the field that goes by the name "business intelligence" for many years, and in my experience this industry has never adhered or lived up to the definition originally provided by Howard Dresner: "Concepts and methods to improve business decision making by using fact-based support systems." [26] Instead, business intelligence has primarily functioned as a name for technologies and processes that are used to collect, store, and produce automated reports of data. Rarely has there been an emphasis on "concepts and methods to improve business decision making," which feature human efforts rather than technologies. This failure of emphasis has resulted in the failure of most business intelligence efforts, which have produced relatively little intelligence.

All of the popular terms that have emerged over the years to describe the work that I and many others do with data, including "decision support," "data warehousing," "analytics," "data science," and of course, "Big Data," have been plagued by definitional dysfunction, leading to confusion and bad practices.

In summary, Big Data fails as a term for two fundamental reasons: 1) it lacks a common core of shared meaning, and 2) it does not clearly distinguish Big Data from data in general. Although it's certainly true that definitions of terms can vary to some degree from dictionary to dictionary and person to person, they share a common core—an essential meaning. Big Data, however, varies significantly in the essential meanings that have been ascribed to it. As such, it has no meaning on which we can rely.

For the concepts, methods, and practices that we engage in to understand data, I prefer the term "data sensemaking." Beginning several years ago, prior to the emergence of "Big Data" as a term, the healthcare sector suggested another useful term—"evidence-based medicine"—to promote the value of data as the raw material from which understanding is woven. This term's generalized form—"evidence-based decision making"—is relatively simple, straightforward, clear, and therefore useful. If we relied on terms such as "data sensemaking" or "evidence-based decision making" to describe what we do when striving to derive value from data, we would waste less time chasing illusions and spend more time focusing on what's fundamentally needed: data-sensemaking skills, augmented by good technologies, to support evidence-based decision making.

Do we really need new terms to promote the importance of this work? Those of us who possess the skills that are needed to glean real value from data don't crave new terms, and we certainly don't relish another distracting and confusing marketing campaign. Rallying those who don't understand data or its use around silly terms such as "Big Data" has certainly led to a great deal of enthusiasm, but that enthusiasm has resulted in an equally great deal of waste and confusion.

CHAPTER 2 – BIG DATA, BIG ILLUSION

No matter which of Big Data's competing definitions you choose, there is no evidence that it actually exists.

To accept Big Data as real is to believe that something substantial and significant about data or its use has changed in recent years. This hasn't happened. Similar to what Gertrude Stein once said about a rose, "data is data is data." Or, to alter a phrase from Shakespeare, "data by any other name would smell as sweet." Data has been rapidly growing in quantity for a very long time. New sources of data have been emerging for a very long time. The ways in which we interact with data today are fundamentally the same ways that we've been interacting with data for a very long time. Nothing worthy of a new name for data or its use has occurred in recent years. We can certainly acknowledge and appreciate specific advances in data and its use without pretending that the landscape has fundamentally shifted. Big Data is an illusion.

On the heels on the previous chapter, "Big Data, Big Confusion," what I'm arguing here in this chapter is that, even if Big Data had a clear meaning, which it doesn't, it wouldn't matter because none of the claims about Big Data are true. Martyn Jones was correct when he wrote, back in 2014:

> *Big Data is dead!...Of course I am overstating. It isn't tangibly dead, because outside of PR and Marketing, and the gullible imaginations of a few punters with more dollars than sense, it was never actually alive.* [1]

Big Data is and has always been an illusion. Gertrude Stein's famous statement about her childhood home in Oakland, California "There is no there there," would be even more accurate if it had been uttered about Big Data. Dan Ariely got it right when he wrote, "Big data is like teenage sex: everyone talks about it, nobody really knows how to do it, everyone thinks everyone else is doing it, so everyone claims they are doing it..." [2] Popularity sometimes breeds ever-increasing popularity even when substance is completely lacking. Big Data and the Kardashians have a lot in common. "But," you might object, "how can something that everyone has been talking about for years be pure fiction?" Marketing campaigns often promote pure fictions and do so unabashedly.

To date, relatively few people have questioned the legitimacy of Big Data, not because its legitimacy is well established but because it's assumed. Try to bring Big Data into focus, and you will find that it dissolves into thin air. The frequency of the term's use is not the result of any real evidence that it exists. Can this much talk about something really grow from a mere assumption of its existence, without any actual evidence? It can and has.

Consider for a moment the question of God's existence. Belief in the existence of one or more gods has long been prolific but not because of any actual evidence. People believe in God because doing so serves their needs, not because they have any proof that God exists. The same is true of Big Data. What's different between Big Data and God, however, is the fact that belief in Big Data only serves the needs of technology vendors and their collaborators, most of whom don't actually share in this belief.

Apart from technology vendors and their collaborators, well-intentioned and otherwise credible people and organizations talk about and promote Big Data without ever questioning its legitimacy. This lends an air of legitimacy to a complete farce. How, you might ask, could the Public Broadcasting System (PBS) talk about Big Data if it weren't real? How could the American Association for the Advancement of Science (AAAS) talk about Big Data if it weren't real? They can and do because they've naïvely assumed its legitimacy without ever questioning it. Big Data is not their area of expertise. People with relevant expertise who endorse Big Data neither assume nor believe its legitimacy. They merely take advantage of the public's naïve belief in Big Data for their own ends.

Let's review the meanings that have been assigned to Big Data—the same meanings that we examined in the previous chapter—along with the claims that are embedded in these meanings to see whether these claims are legitimate.

Data Sets That Are Extremely Large

Large data sets have always existed. There has never been a time during my IT career, which spans nearly 35 years, when we weren't faced with some data sets that seemed overwhelmingly BIG. Although it is true that the data sets we consider big today are often bigger than those that we considered big 30 years ago, 20 years ago, and even 10 years ago, there was no point in recent history when data suddenly began to increase at an unprecedented rate. If a definition of Big Data based on data quantity were meaningful, there would have to be a point in time when the amount of data increased to an extent that changed the nature of data or its use in a substantial way. Otherwise, why invent a new name for data?

In the 1970s, before I began my IT career, people were already talking about *very large database (VLDB)* technologies. Larger-than-usual data sets have always posed a challenge, and efforts have always been made to improve data-handling technologies to address this challenge.

It is true that a few Internet-based organizations such as Google, Facebook, and Twitter amass huge stores of data today, but other organizations have been amassing huge volumes of data for many years. Large retailers, insurance companies, banks, telecommunication companies, and government agencies, to name a few, have also been doing this for a very long time. We can do it with greater ease today than in the past, thanks to gradual advances in technologies, but what we do today is not essentially or substantially different from what we did before.

In the context of Big Data hype, it's worth noting that organizations tend to exaggerate the sizes of their data sets. Slater Victoroff wrote an entertaining and enlightening article about this in 2015. Here's a bit of what he wrote:

> *My customers always lie to me...about how much data they have.*
>
> *...*
>
> *Companies brag about the size of their datasets the way fishermen brag about the size of their fish. They claim access*

to endless terabytes of information. The advantages seem obvious: the more you know, the better... Most companies only have a fraction of the data they claim. And typically, only a small fraction of that fraction is useful for generating any non-trivial insight.

Why do companies lie about the size of their data? Because they want to feel like one of the big dogs. They've heard about the enormous reserves of data collected by the likes of Amazon, Facebook and Google. And even though they don't have the reach to collect that much data—or the money to buy it—they want to feel (and have outsiders think) they are in on the trend.

...

But even big companies only use a tiny fraction of the data they collect.

Big data isn't big, but good data is even smaller.

Twitter processes around 8 terabytes of data per day. That sounds intimidating to a small company trying to extract consumer insights from tweets. But how much of that data is the actual content of tweets? Twitter users create 500 million tweets per day, and the average tweet is 60 characters. If we do the simple math, that's just 30 gigabytes of actual text content per day—about half a percent of 8 terabytes.

The pattern continues. Wikipedia is one of the largest repositories of text on the Internet, but all its text data could fit on a single USB. All the music in the world could fit on a $600 disk drive. I could go on, but the point is this: big data isn't big, but good data is even smaller. [3]

Not everyone who has written about Big Data shares Victoroff's sane perspective. Mayer-Schönberger and Cukier, the authors of *Big Data: A Revolution That Will Transform How We Live, Work, and Think* claim that data has grown so large and so fast that the increase in quantity constitutes a qualitative change of state.

Not only is the world awash with more information than ever before, but that information is growing faster. The change of scale has led to a change of state. The quantitative change has led to a qualitative one. [4]

The essential point about big data is that change of scale leads to change of state. [5]

Many proponents make this claim about Big Data, but I've yet to see anyone substantiate it. Perhaps it is true that some things can grow to such a size and at such a rate that they break through some quantitative barrier into the realm of qualitative change, but what evidence do we have that this has happened with data?

Mayer-Schönberger and Cukier provide many examples of data analytics that have been useful during the past 20 years or so, which they classify as Big Data, but this attribution is contrived. Not one of the examples demonstrates a radical departure from the past. Here's one involving Google:

Big data operates at a scale that transcends our ordinary understanding. For example, the correlation Google identified between a handful of search terms and the flu was the result of testing 450 million mathematical models. [6]

I suspect that Google's discovery of a correlation between search activity and incidents of the flu in particular areas resulted not from 450 million distinct mathematical models, but rather a predictive analytics algorithm making millions of minor adjustments during the process of building a single model. If they really created 450 million different models, or even if they actually made that many manual tweaks to an evolving model to find this relatively simple correlation, is this really an example of progress? A little statistical thinking by a human being could have found this correlation with the help of a computer much more directly. Regardless of how many models were actually used, the final model was not overly complicated. What was done did not transcend the ordinary understanding of data analysts. Also, Google eventually discovered that this particular algorithm was severely flawed, leading the company to abandon it.

And now, for the paradigm-shattering implications of this change of state, according to Mayer-Schönberger and Cukier:

> *Big data is poised to reshape the way we live, work, and think. The change we face is in some ways even greater than those sparked by earlier epochal innovations that dramatically expanded the scope and scale of information in society. The ground beneath our feet is shifting. Old certainties are being questioned. Big data requires fresh discussion of the nature of decision-making, destiny, justice. A worldview we thought was made of causes is being challenged by a preponderance of correlations. The possession of knowledge, which once meant an understanding of the past, is coming to mean an ability to predict the future.* [7]

Does any of this strike you as particularly new? Everything that these authors claim as particular and new to Big Data is in fact old news.

Data has increased in volume at an exponential rate at many points in history. One of the earliest points was the development of language. With the emergence of words to express information came a dramatic increase in data. The invention of writing created another surge. The invention of the printing press another. In the 20th century, the invention of the computer led to another surge, initially with big clunky machines that required entire rooms and then even more dramatically with the introduction of the personal computer. More recently still, the invention of the Internet gradually produced another huge surge in data as the web moved from the exclusive repository of governments and universities to the playground of the entire world. The invention of digital music and images (both photos and movies) caused their own surges. Once the Internet was used by a large portion of the population, social media invited everyone to share personal data. And, more recently still, the so-called "Internet of Things" has put device-generated data, which has been around for ages, on the fast track to even larger data stores.

Each of these information technologies has led to exponential increases in data volume. So, when exactly did data suddenly become big? It didn't. Some data has always seemed big. By that I mean that it has always challenged our ability to glean value from it with ease. With the exception of social media, all of the technologies that have led to surges in exponential rates of increase have existed well in advance of the date when Big Data supposedly emerged.

If Big Data is defined as data that has increased in volume at an unprecedented rate, then Big Data is nothing different from what data has been all along.

Data from Various Sources and of Various Types

In what sense does the emergence of new data sources—something that happens all the time and always has—change the nature of data or its use? In no sense. New data sources are sometimes useful and sometimes not. Most of the data from a new source never amounts to anything but noise. Every new activity creates a new source of data, but newness does not necessarily correlate with usefulness. Collecting and storing every possible source of data is no more productive than collecting and storing every instance of data. More is not necessarily better. In fact, more is usually not better.

Let's consider a recent example. Has the data generated by social media during the past decade changed the nature of data or its use in an unprecedented way? No, unless you wish to argue that the proliferation of data that is of little value constitutes a fundamental change. If we consider the other source of data that has contributed most to increases in volume—digital music and image files—let me ask you a question: Do you ever examine the data files on which digital songs or pictures are based? Of course not because those digital files are not human-readable. We care about the translated results—a beautiful song, photo, or film—but not about the data into which they've been transcribed for use by a computer.

If Big Data is defined as data that comes from new sources, nothing has been introduced in recent years that transformed data into something different than before.

Data That Exhibits High Volume, Velocity, and Variety

Increases in data volume, velocity, and variety have been with us as long as data has been with us. They have not fundamentally changed the nature of data or its use. If, as some have done, you expand the three Vs of volume, velocity, and variety to include a fourth, veracity (truth), Big Data still remains an illusion. However, by adding veracity to the mix, you increase the confusion. Does anyone actually believe that data has suddenly become more truthful? The addition of veracity is only an admission by some proponents of Big Data that data can be harmful if it is erroneous or misused. This is absolutely true—and it always has been.

Data That Is Especially Complex

At what point in history did we not have some data that seemed complex? When did the complexity of data pass some threshold in recent history that sets it apart from previous data? Data that seems complex when gauged by our cognitive abilities has always existed. At no point in recent history did data pass a threshold of complexity that separates it from data in the past. Data has indeed increased in complexity over time; that's a given. As we humans have learned to use our brains in increasingly complex ways, we have created an increasingly complex world. When language emerged and gave us the ability to reason abstractly, this created a huge leap in complexity. When agriculture emerged, leading over many centuries to the creation of huge population centers, life and the systems that supported it had to grow in complexity. When science emerged, it opened our eyes to levels of complexity that had always existed but were previously invisible.

I am not denying the emergence of complex data. I'm saying that it isn't new. New examples of complex data emerge all the time, but they don't change the nature of data or its use in some essential or substantial way. Even if a new source of data emerged that caused substantially new approaches to data sensemaking to be developed and that new source of data deserved a special name to set it apart, Big Data, in all its wondrous vagueness, is not that name.

If Big Data is defined as data that is especially complex, Big Data is still just data.

Data That Is Processed Using Advanced Analytical Methods

Analytical methods that are deemed "advanced"—a relative term—have been around since the beginning of analytical thinking. Most of the methods that are identified as advanced in Big Data definitions today have actually been around for quite some time. For example, even though computers were not always powerful enough to run machine-learning algorithms on large data sets, these algorithms are based on traditional statistical methods or on methods that are derived from them.

Nor has the expertise that is required to process data substantially changed in recent years. Like everything else related to data and its use, data-sensemaking skills increase among individuals with study and experience and thus gradually increase cumulatively in the world as a whole but not in a manner that corresponds to the emergence of Big Data as a term. If Big Data actually corresponded to a substantially greater emphasis on the development of data-sensemaking skills, I would be inclined to embrace it, but the opposite has occurred. The emergence of Big Data has corresponded to a greater emphasis on technologies as the agents of data sensemaking, with skilled humans taking a back seat to machines.

If Big Data is defined as advanced analytical methods, Big Data is nothing more than a continuation of the past.

Any Data at All That Is Associated with a Current Fad

At a time when people consider data to be the new oil fueling our economy, fads related to data and its use are rife. That's not surprising. Some of these might turn out to be more than fads, and, if they do, it would be reasonable to acknowledge their benefits and promote their use. For instance, machine learning, despite excessive hype and a general misunderstanding of what it actually is, provides real value when applied appropriately and with skill. As such, we should call it what it is—machine learning—not Big Data. Lending credence to Big Data by inappropriately associating it with other things that deserve respect is a deceitful ploy.

To summarize, none of the claims that people associate with Big Data to separate it from data of the past are true. Nothing has occurred in recent years that warrants a new term for data and its use. In Big Data, there really is no there there.

CHAPTER 3 – BIG DATA, BIG RUSE

Big Data is nothing but a marketing campaign that was designed to put money in the pockets of technology vendors and their collaborators.

So, if Big Data is an illusion, why do so many people talk as if it's real? The answer is simple: Big Data is an extraordinarily successful marketing campaign. It is big money for IT product and service providers. It has also been very lucrative for the industry analysts, so-called thought leaders, and pseudo-journalists who make a living by promoting these technology providers.

I'm not aware of any software vendor in the data analytics space that hasn't hitched its wagon to Big Data. The vendors never question the concept, nor do they struggle with the ethical implications of promoting an illusion. And there is a dirty little secret that none of these beneficiaries of the Big Data hype will admit. Except for those who haven't been around long enough to know better, most of these folks don't themselves drink the Kool-Aid that they sell to their customers. They know that they're selling a rebranded continuation of the past.

Rebranding as a Source of Revenues

In the realm of information technologies, new terms for the same things emerge every few years to revive interest and thus sales. Over the course of my career, the terms "decision support," "data warehousing," "business intelligence," "analytics," "Big Data," and, even more recently, "data science" have all described the same domain: using data to gain understanding and support sound decisions. The purveyors of the technologies associated with each of these concepts always act as if each reframing is brand new even though there are often no corresponding changes to the products and services. Every new rebranding promises a solution, at last, to the perpetual problems that plague us today as much as they did when my career began over 30 years ago.

This situation brings to mind the lesson that Jesus taught using the parable of the wine skins:

> *No one pours new wine into old wineskins. If he does, the wine will burst the skins, and both the wine and the wineskins will be ruined. No, he pours new wine into new wineskins.* [1]

The fermentation of new wine requires a vessel that can expand. New wineskins were flexible, but old wineskins no longer had the capacity for expansion. Jesus was saying that his message was new—a departure from the past—and that it could not be contained within the rigid, confining paradigms of the past. It was qualitatively different, and as such, following him would require a new perspective. The flip side of this parable is what comes to mind when I think of Big Data. Only marketers (people who are trying to sell you something) pour old wine into new wineskins. This is the essence of rebranding. Doing so wastes the capacity of the new wineskins, because expansion isn't needed, and misleads buyers into thinking that they're getting something new that is actually old. Big Data isn't new.

In his book, *Big Data at Work*, Thomas Davenport directly acknowledged this problem when he wrote, "It is a well-established phenomenon that vendors and consultants will take any new, hot term and apply it to their existing offerings—and that has already happened in spades with big data." [2] Unfortunately, after bemoaning this fact, Davenport proceeded to write an entire book about Big Data as if it were new. The entire chapter in his book titled "Developing a Big Data Strategy" lays out a plan for doing exactly what organizations have attempted to do for ages: discovering useful insights in data and putting them to use as "cost savings," "faster decisions," "better decisions," or "product/service innovation." [3]

Big Data is like the Borg of *Star Trek: The Next Generation*. The Borg, a hybrid race of humans and machines, tries to assimilate all sentient beings in its path into the collective Borg mind. This is what marketing campaigns do when they claim everything of value as their own and then sell that vision as novel and essential, even though they aren't providing anything new or useful. Davenport admits and bemoans this problem:

> *Big data is undeniably big, but it's also a bit misnamed. It's a catchall term for data that doesn't fit the usual containers.* [4]

In another chapter of Davenport's book titled "Technology for Big Data"—one written by Jill Dyché—several admissions are made about the old nature of Big Data. Davenport believes that Big Data differs from data of the past mostly in that much of it is unstructured, but when writing about unstructured data and the tools that we use to analyze data, Dyché said:

> *These approaches for converting unstructured data into structured numbers are not entirely new either. For as long as we've been analyzing text, voice, and video data, for example, we've had to convert it into numbers for analysis...The only thing that's new about it is the speed and cost with which this conversion can be accomplished. It's important to remember, however, that such a conversion isn't useful until data are summarized, analyzed, and correlated through analytics.*
>
> *The tools that organizations use for big data analysis aren't that different from what has been used for data analysis in the past. They include basic statistical processing with either proprietary (e.g., SAS or SPSS) or open-source (e.g., R) statistical programs.* [5]

What Dyché wrote here is true, yet these words appear in a book that was marketed as essential reading for organizations that don't want to be left behind.

One vivid example of the rebranding ploy—one that chaps my hide—is a silly little book titled *The Big Data Revolution*, published by Jason Kolb and Jeremy Kolb in 2013. Actually, on the cover of the book, the title is preceded by the words "Secrets of." The authors promise early on, "This book is your guidebook—your map—telling you where you need to go and what you need to do to exploit this unique opportunity." [6] This guidance is supposedly so special, "your competitors do not want you to read this book." [7]

> No matter what business you are looking to get into, you'll find that there are secrets about it insiders just don't want to reveal. Little tricks that make it seem like they are doing something truly magical, and if you don't know what's happening behind the scenes, then it is [sic] absolutely seems like magic to you. It's no different in the data industry. [8]

What are these secrets? The book rehashes the same old stories that have been told for many years. Business Intelligence is rebranded as a confusing mixture of data science, data intelligence, data discovery, and, of course, Big Data. What are the new big challenges of Big Data? "Get the data, manage it, and understand it." [9] The same old challenges. The exciting new tools of this revolution "are built to empower the end-user to investigate on his own in real-time (or close to it). If you see something interesting you can drill into it immediately and continue to iterate in that way." [10] This is hardly new. According to the authors, however, it contrasts with the "traditional approach which is for information consumers to ask questions, which causes reports to be developed, which are then fed to the consumer, which may generate more questions, which will generate more reports." [11] This marketing claim that we are suddenly abandoning lackluster reports for instant insights is one that has been made in the data industry throughout my career. We are constantly being told that we're abandoning those dry reports for the latest analytical magic, but the reports persist nonetheless.

With inspiration from the futuristic vision of Tom Cruise navigating data at the speed of thought in the movie *Minority Report*, the authors reveal an emerging age when "the ability to use analytics will no longer be a specialized skill," but instead "will be a common and everyday thing for executives on down the line to use as part of their daily and hourly workflow." [12]

This book is pure marketing drivel from the first page to the last. And speaking of the last, upon reaching the last page without finding any of the Big Data secrets that were promised, I read the final section heading: "You found the secret page." I kid you not. And what did the secret page reveal? The book's real purpose: an announcement that the authors were working on a "brand new product...that makes getting value out of your data easier than it's ever been." [13] The product, called Touchdata, is—you guessed it—"revolutionary." Don't bother looking for the product. If it was ever released, it didn't last long. In fact, the authors' company, Applied Data Labs, no longer exists either. Unfortunately, while they were still in business, they were luring people into believing the ruse of Big Data.

The purpose of the term "Big Data" as it's being used by technology vendors and most technology thought leaders is to create an illusion of something new that potential buyers can't live without. The term is a marketing campaign designed to do one thing: fatten the wallets of technology vendors and their collaborators. An organization that cannot derive value from the data that it already has will not suddenly derive value from it or any other data merely by installing the latest technology. The Big Data industry and its predecessors have always been good at making the same old rarely fulfilled promises.

The Allure of All Things Big

I guess it shouldn't be surprising that sticking the word "big" in front of "data" turned out to be a formula for marketing success. It is our base nature to crave everything that comes in mega-sizes. In data, as in food, this is a recipe for indigestion and a path to obesity. Big Data is a technological expression of gluttony. An unhealthy appetite for increasingly more data is like an insatiable craving for wealth or entertainment. Beyond a certain level, further acquisition is useless. It doesn't make us happier and it certainly doesn't make us better people (or organizations). The constant pursuit of more turns us into obsessive hoarders, slaves to our appetites. Only a productive use of the right data will lead to healthy outcomes that satisfy. This truth is not sexy, however, and therefore it isn't popular.

A Network of Collusion

The claims about Big Data are designed to channel big revenues to Big Data's purveyors and the companies that derive benefits from supporting them, including consultancies and industry analysts. Here's a typical example from McKinsey Global Institute (MGI):

> MGI studied big data in five domains—healthcare in the United States, the public sector in Europe, retail in the United States, and manufacturing and personal-location data globally. Big data can generate value in each. For example, a retailer using big data to the full could increase its operating margin by more than 60 percent. Harnessing big data in the public sector has enormous potential, too. If US healthcare were to use big data creatively and effectively to drive efficiency and quality, the sector could create more than $300 billion in value every year. Two-thirds of that would be in the form of reducing US healthcare expenditure by about 8 percent. In the developed economies of Europe, government administrators could save more than 100 billion euros ($149 billion) in operational efficiency improvements alone by using big data, not including using big data to reduce fraud and errors and boost the collection of tax revenues. And users of services enabled by personal-location data could capture $600 billion in consumer surplus. [14]

You might be willing to trust such claims as a 60% increase in operating margin, a $300 billion annual increase in value, an 8% reduction in expenditures, or a $600 billion consumer surplus, but don't embarrass yourself by trying to quantify these benefits after spending millions of dollars on Big Data technologies. You'll surely fail. No one attempts to confirm the fantastical claims of Big Data. After spending all of that money, time, and effort, which could have been spent more productively, no one willingly audits the results of Big Data's promises. To do so would be an admission of utter foolishness and failure.

Despite an ugly landscape of botched projects, the marketing engine continues to churn out drivel. Bernard Marr, an independent "thought leader" who serves as a marketing extension of Big Data technology vendors, wrote the following in 2014:

> *Big data is moving on. We're moving past the stage where it's something only trailblazers and early adopters are on board with, towards a time when if you aren't analyzing data to help you make better business decisions, you're in danger of being left behind.*
>
> ...
>
> *A couple of years ago, when big data was very much the "word of the moment" in business circles, there were people who were suspicious it was just a passing trend. That it could simply be another fad for shady consultants to make a quick buck out of credulous businessmen eager not to miss the "next big thing."*
>
> *The last couple of years have proved them spectacularly wrong. Now that it exists, big data is simply too good a concept to do away with.* [15]

Be still, my beating heart. This is outlandish, self-serving nonsense, and Marr must certainly know it. Either that or he's genuinely deluded. Regardless, he has plenty of company. A lot of back-slapping is going on as Marr and many, many others like him celebrate their good fortune.

Follow the Money

To understand the true nature of Big Data, we need only follow the money. Who benefits financially? Consider Big Data's self-serving assumption that we can and should collect every bit of data that's produced in the world just in case it might prove useful at some point in the future. In their book *Big Data: A Revolution That Will*

Transform How We Live, Work, and Think, Mayer-Schönberger and Cukier make the following arguments:

> *Discarding data may have been appropriate when the cost and complexity of collecting, storing, and analyzing it were high, but this is no longer the case.* [16]

> *Every single dataset is likely to have some intrinsic, hidden, not yet unearthed value, and the race is on to discover and capture all of it.* [17]

> *Data's true value is like an iceberg floating in the ocean. Only a tiny part of it is visible at first sight, while much of it is hidden beneath the surface.* [18]

We can certainly find new uses for data that was originally generated for another purpose, such as transaction data that we later use for analytical purposes to improve decisions, but in the past we rarely collected data primarily for potential secondary uses. Perhaps this is a characteristic that actually qualifies as new. Regardless, we must ask the question, "Is this a viable business model?" Should all organizations begin collecting and retaining more data in hope of finding unforeseen secondary uses for it in the future? I find it hard to imagine that secondary uses of data will provide enough benefit to warrant collecting everything and keeping it forever, as the authors seem to believe. Despite the argument that collecting everything is a no-brainer based on decreasing hardware costs, the price is actually quite high because it is not based on the cost of hardware alone.

Imagine the time that will be wasted and the cost of such a data-collection effort. Only a tiny fraction of data that is being generated today will ever be valuable beyond its original use. A few nuggets of gold might exist in that iceberg below the water line, but do we really need to collect and save it all? Even Mayer-Schönberger and Cukier admit concern about this.

> *Most data loses some of it utility over time. In such circumstances, continuing to rely on old data doesn't just fail to add value; it actually destroys the value of fresher data.* [19]

Collecting, storing, and retaining everything will make it harder and harder to focus on the little that actually has value. Nevertheless, Mayer-Schönberger and Cukier predict that the prize will go to those with the most.

> *Scale still matters, but it has shifted…What counts is scale in data. This means holding large pools of data and being able to capture even more of it with ease. Thus large data holders will flourish as they gather and store more of the raw material of their business, which they can reuse to create additional value.* [20]

If this were true, wouldn't the organizations with the most data today be the most successful? This isn't the case. In fact, many organizations with the most data are drowning in it. I know, because I've tried to help them change this dynamic. Having lots of data is useless unless you know how to make sense of it and how to apply what you learn.

We are peering at tea leaves, trying to find meaning in soggy green clumps. Unforeseen uses for data certainly exist, but they are, by definition, difficult to anticipate. Do we really want to collect, store, and retain everything possible on the off chance that it might be useful? Who benefits from our commitment to collect and store all of the data that's produced?

- The companies that make the hardware and software that are required to achieve this goal
- The companies that provide storage facilities in the cloud
- The companies that produce much of the data that is now being heralded as critical, including social media companies such as Facebook and search companies such as Google
- The consultancies that provide the workers who are required to make this proposition functional
- The thought leaders and industry analysts who earn a living by promoting the interests of these companies

And who are the most vocal advocates of Big Data? You guessed it: these very same companies and individuals.

Collecting and storing everything has a high cost. If we proceed according to this dictum of Big Data, only a tiny fraction of that cost will ever be justified. Not everyone will bear this cost. In fact, a few companies and individuals will benefit to the degree that the rest of us suffer.

At a time when America is governed by a President who substitutes boasts for ability and "alternative facts" for truth, it shouldn't surprise us that organizations exhibit the gullibility that Big Data demands. Trumpery, which meant deceit, fraud, trickery, and worthless nonsense long before the rise of its namesake Donald Trump, has replaced good sense and truth. In the name of good-old-fashioned marketing, technology vendors and their collaborators are laughing all the way to the bank as organizations subject to the vagaries of Big Data languish in a deluge of data despair. I have no respect for an industry to treats its customers like rubes. You shouldn't either.

CHAPTER 4 – BIG DATA, BIG DISTRACTION

Pursuing Big Data distracts us from doing what's actually needed to derive value from data.

Although the meaning of Big Data is unclear, the essential message that it promotes is not. According to its advocates, you cannot survive without massive amounts of data and so-called Big Data technologies and techniques. Big Data proponents encourage investments of time and money that are seldom needed or useful. As such, Big Data is an expensive distraction. Organizations have only so much time and money. Investing in Big Data is an expensive way to divert funds from the investments needed to derive value from data.

Successful uses of data cannot be measured in petabytes or any other unit of data volume. Success must be measured as increases in understanding and the better decisions that result from that understanding. Just because we can generate and collect more data doesn't mean we should. Martyn Jones got it right when he wrote: "We neither can nor should we strive to analyze everything, and such claims only serve to highlight the crass manipulation that is associated with this tsunami of fatuous and malignant hype." [1]

Several specific technologies have been associated with Big Data, none more than Hadoop. Initially released in 2008, according to its caretaker, the Apache Software Foundation, Hadoop "is a framework that allows for the distributed processing of large data sets across clusters of computers using simple programming models. It is designed to scale up from single servers to thousands of machines, each offering local computation and storage." In other words, Hadoop is a modern database engine. It is considered a Big Data technology merely because of timing; both emerged at about the same time. Designed to manage the demands of large data sets, Hadoop is certainly useful for the relatively few organizations that face this challenge. When Hadoop is useful, it can be implemented without any concern whatsoever for Big Data. Any success that is achieved by using Hadoop should not be attributed to Big Data but instead to the fine software engineers who developed it. The same applies to all products that have been marketed as Big Data technologies.

Signal and Noise

Most data is noise. This will always be the case. As the haystacks of data grow, it becomes harder to find needles of meaning within them. Nassim N. Taleb said in *Wired*:

> *We're more fooled by noise than ever before, and it's because of a nasty phenomenon called "big data." With big data, researchers have brought cherry-picking to an industrial level… But beyond that, big data means anyone can find fake statistical relationships, since the spurious rises to the surface. This is because in large data sets, large deviations are vastly more attributable to variance (or noise) than to information (or signal).* [2]

You could record data about every blink of your eyes, but would that be useful? Unless you're a scientist studying eye blinking, the answer is "No." Even if it were useful, you would need to take great care to find any signals.

Here's the inconvenient truth that must be acknowledged but seldom is: until you've figured out how to use the data that you already have, collecting more is a harmful distraction. Time spent collecting more data is time that could be better spent weaving it into something meaningful. Back in 1939, the poet Edna St. Vincent Millay was prescient when she wrote:

> *Upon this gifted age, in its dark hour,*
> *rains from the sky a meteoric shower*
> *of facts…they lie, unquestioned, uncombined.*
> *Wisdom enough to leach us of our ill*
> *is daily spun; but there exists no loom*
> *to weave it into a fabric.* [3]

As data is accumulating at a feverish pace, the corpses of failed opportunities are piling up. Time spent keeping your head above water is time that could have been spent working productively with data. More data rarely results in more understanding and even more rarely in greater wisdom. Understanding and wisdom are the only outcomes worth pursuing.

A Typical Big Data Scenario

Consider a typical Big Data scenario. You manage a company that, like most others, must rely on data to be informed and make good decisions. Despite living in the so-called "information age," your efforts over the last 30 years have had little success. You're frustrated. What are you missing? Years ago you invested in data warehousing technologies and built several large data repositories. Your organization never derived much value from them, however. Most have since been abandoned. A few years later you heard about business intelligence (BI), the new technological messiah, and invested time and effort to put a BI infrastructure into place. You now have hundreds of production reports, but few are actually used, and fewer still provide benefit when they are. People spend their days wading through data with little reward. They don't know what they're looking for and probably wouldn't be able to find it in their reports if they did.

Why have your well-intentioned, industrious efforts failed so miserably? The answer, you're now told, is that, in contrast to your previous efforts, what you really need is Big Data. The irony—the fact that this answer is coming from the same technology vendors that previously sold you on the promises of data warehousing and BI—never occurs to you. You also fail to notice that your actions are illustrating the dictum usually attributed to Albert Einstein: "The definition of insanity is doing the same thing over and over and expecting different results." Big Data is different from BI and data warehousing and isn't just more of the same—right? After all, if it were, surely it wouldn't be called by a different name.

Once again, your organization spends millions of dollars and years of effort to install products with new names that proudly wave the glorious banner of Big Data. Even though learning these new products feels like learning something entirely different, what they do is essentially the same as the products that you used in the past.

Where does all this time, effort, and money get you? Nowhere useful. It is a costly distraction. If you consider the opportunities that you've lost, you find yourself not just back where you began but further behind than ever. That is, you would find this to be true if you ever bothered to assess the situation, which is almost never done.

This is the story of Big Data as it is experienced by most organizations that buy into its promises. If you personally made the decision to make this investment, it's unlikely that you'll ever admit its failure. Due to cognitive dissonance, you'll be inclined to just move on eventually to another iteration of this sad story when Big Data is replaced by the next clever marketing campaign. It won't be difficult to hide your failure because the outcomes of your Big Data efforts will never be investigated. And so the story goes from one generation of failure to the next.

This is a sad story. It breaks my heart.

Distraction from What's Needed

What's especially sad is the fact that this story isn't inevitable. The potential of data as the source of understanding and better decisions is real but seldom tapped. The path to achieving this is the road less travelled. Why? Because the sure path to success isn't sexy, and it isn't easy. It requires a commitment that few people and organizations are willing to make.

Tapping into the potential of data involves data sensemaking. I prefer this term over the more popular term "analytics" because it better fits the full range of activities that are needed. Making sense of data requires more than analysis, which, strictly speaking, is the act of breaking data down into its component parts. Digging into the details is only one of many tasks that we perform to understand data. The full range of data-sensemaking activities requires skills that few of those who are tasked with the effort take time to acquire. Most people in data-sensemaking roles have learned what they know on the job, and it rarely consists of more than the ability to use a particular tool (Excel, Power BI, Tableau, etc.). Most of those with more extensive skills have only added a little statistical training to the mix. Training in statistics is vital, but that alone produces a myopic approach to data. In addition to statistics, data sensemaking involves several other thinking skills, including critical thinking, logical thinking, scientific thinking, visual thinking (applied as data visualization), systems thinking, and even ethical thinking. Beyond these thinking skills, data sensemakers must also become skilled in clear communication because their work is useless unless the decision makers who rely on them can understand their findings.

The skills needed for data sensemaking can only be developed through extensive training and practice. How many organizations adequately support the development of data-sensemaking skills? The answer, in my experience, is almost none. Instead, organizations invest their time and resources in chasing the latest technologies, placing their faith in elusive and illusory promises that technologies alone can never deliver. Data sensemaking is primarily a human activity, not one that machines can perform. At best, technologies can assist us in this work. This truth is rarely recognized. It is certainly not a message that you've ever heard from a technology company.

Richards J. Heuer, Jr. argued in the *Psychology of Intelligence Analysis* (1999) that the primary failures of data sensemaking are not due to insufficient data but to flawed thinking. Heuer spent 45 years supporting the work of the Central Intelligence Agency (CIA). Identifying a potential threat might require an intelligence analyst to sift through a lot of data, but more importantly, it relies on the analyst's ability to connect the dots. In sharp contrast to Heuer's emphasis on thinking skills, Big Data emphasizes more, more, and more data.

Successful data sensemakers will tell you that data sensemaking requires both broad and deep skills. Tools don't make a data sensemaker. Rather than the road less traveled, however, technology vendors and their collaborators encourage magical thinking, the yellow brick road to the Emerald City. Oh, if only life were so simple! Until people and organizations embrace the truth that data's bounty will only be reaped through great effort, they will remain impoverished. Big Data is just the latest edition of the sad reality of marketing that leads us away from rather than toward what we really need in order to make sense of data.

CHAPTER 5 – BIG DATA, BIG REGRESSION

**Many of Big Data's claims lead us backwards into a
less-enlightened age.**

In 2009, an article appeared in *Nature* that paved the way for the
Big Data marketing campaign that would soon unfold. Titled
"Detecting influenza epidemics using search engine query data," [1]
the authors chronicled how one of Google's algorithms was able to
detect a flu epidemic almost immediately, days before the Centers
for Disease Control (CDC) became aware of it. Cheers went up for
benefits of large data sets mined by automated algorithms.
Unfortunately, the enthusiasm that ensued led to claims that
challenged the very foundations of well-established analytical
principles and practices. The article was used to challenge three
maxims of analytical practice, in particular.

1. *To fully understand and make use of correlations, we must
   understand the nature of cause.* This was challenged by the
   claim that correlations in large data sets alone could and
   should be used without concern for their causes. There's no
   reason to waste our time any longer looking for causes. Simply
   find correlations and act upon them.
2. *Statistical sampling, done properly, can serve as a substitute for
   entire data sets.* This was challenged by the claim that
   sampling was no longer needed because entire data sets could
   and should always be collected and stored.
3. *Data should be approached using scientific methods and can be
   understood using statistical models.* This was challenged by the
   claim that science and statistical models were no longer
   needed because data could now speak for itself.

Other advocates of Big Data have challenged additional analytical principles and practices:

4. *Data is only useful if it is of high quality.* This has been challenged by the claim that with huge data sets, concerns for data quality are eliminated because quantity overcomes the ill effects of erroneous data.
5. *Subject matter expertise is required to fully understand data.* This has been challenged by the claim that expertise is only needed when you don't have enough data.

These challenges to established principles and practices are nonsense. By embracing them, we would step back into the less-enlightened time before the advent of science and statistics. Nevertheless, these silly and regressive claims have captured a great deal of attention.

David Spiegelhalter of Cambridge University is one of the conscientious statisticians who has spoken out against these spurious claims, calling them "complete bollocks...absolute nonsense." According to Spiegelhalter,

> There are a lot of small data problems that occur in big data...They don't disappear because you've got lots of the stuff. They get worse. [2]

Amen to that. Let's consider each of the five regressive assumptions that Big Data is guilty of promoting.

Assumption #1: Causation No Longer Matters

In an excellent article titled "Big data: are we making a big mistake?", Tim Harford critiqued the original *Nature* article that served as the catalyst for the nonsense claim that we no longer need to understand causation:

> Four years after the original Nature *paper was published,* Nature News *had sad tidings to convey: the latest flu outbreak had claimed an unexpected victim: Google Flu Trends. After reliably providing a swift and accurate account of flu outbreaks for several winters, the theory-free, data-rich*

*model had lost its nose for where flu was going. Google's
model pointed to a severe outbreak but when the slow-and-
steady data from the CDC arrived, they showed that Google's
estimates of the spread of flu-like illnesses were overstated by
almost a factor of two.*

*The problem was that Google did not know—could not begin
to know—what linked the search terms with the spread of
flu. Google's engineers weren't trying to figure out what
caused what. They were merely finding statistical patterns in
the data. They cared about correlation rather than causation.
This is common in big data analysis. Figuring out what
causes what is hard (impossible, some say). Figuring out
what is correlated with what is much cheaper and easier...*

*Statisticians have spent the past 200 years figuring out what
traps lie in wait when we try to understand the world through
data. The data are bigger, faster and cheaper these days—but
we must not pretend that the traps have all been made safe.
They have not.* [3]

In their book *Big Data: A Revolution That Will Transform How We
Live, Work, and Think,* Mayer-Schönberger and Cukier contributed to
the notion that Big Data banishes concern about causation: "The
ideal of identifying causal mechanisms is a self-congratulatory
illusion; big data overturns this." [4] This notion scares the hell out of
me. We cannot rely upon and use correlations until we recognize
the causal mechanisms that explain them.

   We progress by seeking and finding ever better explanations for
reality—*what* it is, *how* it works, and *why*. Explanations—the
commitment to finding them and the process of developing and
confirming them—are the essence of science. By rebelling against
authority as the basis of knowledge, the historical period known as
the Enlightenment began the only sustained era of progress that
our species has ever known (see *The Beginning of Infinity,* by David
Deutsch). Trust in established authority was replaced by science, a
search for testable explanations. The information technologies of
today are a result of this search for explanations. To say that we
should begin to rely on correlations alone without concern for

causation encourages a return to the age of ignorance that preceded the advent of science. Prior to science, we lived in a world of myth. We craved explanations but lacked the means to uncover them, so we fabricated explanations that provided comfort or that maintained the control of those in power. To say that explanations are altogether unnecessary today in the world of Big Data holds no hope for the future. Making use of correlations without understanding causation might be useful at times, but it isn't progress, and it is prone to error. Manipulation of reality without understanding is a formula for disaster.

Mayer-Schönberger and Cukier pressed their case to an even greater degree of absurdity when they wrote:

> *Correlations are powerful not only because they offer insights, but also because the insights they offer are relatively clear. These insights often get obscured when we bring causality back into the picture.* [5]

Actually, thinking in terms of causality is the only way that correlations can be fully understood and utilized with confidence. Only when we understand the *why* (cause) can we intelligently leverage our understanding of the *what* (correlation). This is essential to science.

The initial and primary impetus for Big Data arguments in favor of using correlations without understanding their causes was an article written by Chris Anderson in *Wired Magazine* in 2008. It bore the provocative title "The End of Theory: The Data Deluge Makes the Scientific Method Obsolete." Here's an excerpt:

> *This is a world where massive amounts of data and applied mathematics replace every other tool that might be brought to bear. Out with every theory of human behavior, from linguistics to sociology. Forget taxonomy, ontology, and psychology. Who knows why people do what they do? The point is they do it, and we can track and measure it with unprecedented fidelity. With enough data, the numbers speak for themselves.* [6]

Furthermore,

> *There is now a better way. Petabytes allow us to say:*
> *"Correlation is enough." We can stop looking for models. We*
> *can analyze the data without hypotheses about what it might*
> *show. We can throw the numbers into the biggest computing*
> *clusters the world has ever seen and let statistical algorithms*
> *find patterns where science cannot. [7]*

According to Anderson, petabytes are game-changing: "The
Petabyte Age is different because more is different." Except, it isn't.
More is not different. We seem to be suffering from a new delu-
sional disorder—"Petaphilia"—an inordinate love for exceptionally
large data sets. More data does not alter the path to understanding.

Assumption #2: We Don't Need to Use Statistical Samples

Statistical sampling techniques were developed and refined through
many years of work to produce reliable findings when full data sets
were not available. Despite advocates' claims to the contrary, Big
Data does not eliminate the usefulness of statistical samples, and
this is often true even when much larger data sets are available.
About this, Tim Harford wrote the following:

> *In 1936, the Republican Alfred Landon stood for election*
> *against President Franklin Delano Roosevelt. The respected*
> *magazine,* The Literary Digest, *shouldered the responsibility*
> *of forecasting the result. It conducted a postal opinion poll of*
> *astonishing ambition, with the aim of reaching 10 million*
> *people, a quarter of the electorate. The deluge of mailed-in*
> *replies can hardly be imagined but the Digest seemed to be*
> *relishing the scale of the task. In late August it reported,*
> *"Next week, the first answers from these ten million will*
> *begin the incoming tide of marked ballots, to be triple-*
> *checked, verified, five-times cross-classified and totaled."*

After tabulating an astonishing 2.4 million returns as they flowed in over two months, The Literary Digest *announced its conclusions: Landon would win by a convincing 55 per cent to 41 per cent, with a few voters favouring a third candidate.*

The election delivered a very different result: Roosevelt crushed Landon by 61 per cent to 37 per cent. To add to The Literary Digest's *agony, a far smaller survey conducted by the opinion poll pioneer George Gallup came much closer to the final vote, forecasting a comfortable victory for Roosevelt. Mr. Gallup understood something that* The Literary Digest *did not. When it comes to data, size isn't everything.*

Opinion polls are based on samples of the voting population at large. This means that opinion pollsters need to deal with two issues: sample error and sample bias.

Sample error reflects the risk that, purely by chance, a randomly chosen sample of opinions does not reflect the true views of the population. The "margin of error" reported in opinion polls reflects this risk and the larger the sample, the smaller the margin of error. A thousand interviews is a large enough sample for many purposes and Mr. Gallup is reported to have conducted 3,000 interviews.

But if 3,000 interviews were good, why weren't 2.4 million far better? The answer is that sampling error has a far more dangerous friend: sampling bias. Sampling error is when a randomly chosen sample doesn't reflect the underlying population purely by chance; sampling bias is when the sample isn't randomly chosen at all. George Gallup took pains to find an unbiased sample because he knew that was far more important than finding a big one.

The Literary Digest, *in its quest for a bigger data set, fumbled the question of a biased sample. It mailed out forms to people on a list it had compiled from automobile registrations and telephone directories – a sample that, at least in 1936, was disproportionately prosperous. To compound the*

*problem, Landon supporters turned out to be more likely to
mail back their answers. The combination of those two
biases was enough to doom* The Literary Digest's *poll. For
each person George Gallup's pollsters interviewed,* The
Literary Digest *received 800 responses. All that gave them
for their pains was a very precise estimate of the wrong
answer.*

The big data craze threatens to be The Literary Digest *all
over again. Because found data sets are so messy, it can be
hard to figure out what biases lurk inside them—and because
they are so large, some analysts seem to have decided the
sampling problem isn't worth worrying about. It is.* [8]

Assumption #3: We No Longer Need Scientific Method and Models

Scientific method consists of several principles and practices that
have proven useful and reliable. For this reason, some speak of
scientific methods in the plural. Some advocates of Big Data have
predicted the demise of science as obsolete. All such claims that I've
found apparently derived this notion from Chris Anderson's article
in *Wired Magazine*. If you inspect these claims, you'll find that they
typically challenge a particular aspect of scientific method: the
generation and testing of hypotheses. They argue that when you
have all of the data, the understanding that science seeks to acquire
through the generation and testing of hypotheses can be more
readily and directly accessed merely by examining the data. They
fall prey to the erroneous notion that data can speak for itself,
which Anderson boldly claimed. As Michael Malak pointed out in
his Data Science Association blog in 2014, these arguments suggest
that "relying on theory and relying on data are opposites." [9] They
are not. Malak went on to astutely point out,

> *The scientific method advances human knowledge by using
> data to derive theory. Data without theory is fine only under
> 2008 Big Data theories of "collect the data and the insights
> come automatically."* [10]

Data sets have always played a role in science. It is through observations made while examining data that the ideas arise that are then formally expressed as hypotheses—statements of what appears to be true—which are then tested experimentally. Repeated testing of hypotheses that reveals a consistent pattern in outcomes becomes the basis for theories.

Provocative claims often garner a great deal of attention. Many people take pleasure in seeing prevailing wisdom knocked from its pedestal. Anderson concluded his article with the following two sentences:

> There's no reason to cling to our old ways. It's time to ask: What can science learn from Google? [11]

Once again, Google's algorithms applied to massive amounts of data are cited as the new path to understanding. Anderson's article is a vivid example of *technological solutionism*, a term that was coined by Evgeny Morozov to describe our over-reliance on technologies to save the day. In fact, it is one of technological solutionism's most popular manifestos. It is not only utterly naïve, it is downright dangerous. James Bridle pointed this out in his article, "What's wrong with big data?" which appeared in the *New Humanist* on November 1, 2016. What I call "technological solutionism," he calls "technological determinism." Bridle expressed concern about the insidious dangers of Big Data and exposed the invalid nature of its case against science.

> This belief in the power of data, of technology untrammeled by petty human worldviews, is the practical cousin of more metaphysical assertions. A belief in the unquestionability of data leads directly to a belief in the truth of data-derived assertions. And if data contains truth, then it will, without moral intervention, produce better outcomes. Speaking at Google's private London Zeitgeist conference in 2013, Eric Schmidt, Google Chairman, asserted that "if they had had cellphones in Rwanda in 1994, the genocide would not have happened." Schmidt's claim was that technological visibility—the rendering of events and actions legible to everyone— would change the character of those actions. Not only is this

statement historically inaccurate (there was plenty of evidence available of what was occurring during the genocide from UN officials, US satellite photographs and other sources), it's also demonstrably untrue. Analysis of unrest in Kenya in 2007, when over 1,000 people were killed in ethnic conflicts, showed that mobile phones not only spread but accelerated the violence. But you don't need to look to such extreme examples to see how a belief in technological determinism underlies much of our thinking and reasoning about the world. [12]

Anderson's argument targeted scientific models in particular. In fact, he began with an oft-quoted statement by the statistician George Box in a 1979 technical report titled "Robustness in the Strategy of Scientific Model Building": "All models are wrong but some are useful." These words are often ascribed meaning that Box never gave them. These words appeared as a section heading in his report, which went on to say:

Now it would be very remarkable if any system existing in the real world could be exactly represented by any simple model. However, cunningly chosen parsimonious models often do provide remarkably useful approximations...For such a model there is no need to ask the question "Is the model true?". If "truth" is to be the "whole truth" the answer must be "No". The only question of interest is "Is the model illuminating and useful?". [13]

Box wasn't dismissing scientific models in his report, he was suggesting ways to improve them.

In his article "Big data: are we making a big mistake?" Tim Harford addressed this issue as well.

But big data do not solve the problem that has obsessed statisticians and scientists for centuries: the problem of insight, of inferring what is going on, and figuring out how we might intervene to change a system for the better.

...

To use big data to produce such answers will require large strides in statistical methods.

"It's the wild west right now," says Patrick Wolfe of UCL. "People who are clever and driven will twist and turn and use every tool to get sense out of these data sets, and that's cool. But we're flying a little bit blind at the moment."

Statisticians are scrambling to develop new methods to seize the opportunity of big data. Such new methods are essential but they will work by building on the old statistical lessons, not by ignoring them. [14]

To claim that Big Data eliminates the usefulness of models reveals a misunderstanding of their role. It also reveals ignorance of the way in which our brains work. Thinking involves models—some explicit but most implicit—that are built through experience. We cannot think without models. For this reason, if for no other, we will not abandon the construction and reliance on models. We don't build models for lack of data; we build them to represent, in comprehensible ways, the meanings, relationships, and patterns that we discover in data. Models achieve this by reducing something that we learn to its essence and expressing that essence as simply as possible. If anything, models become even more valuable when they are applied to larger and more complex data sets.

Assumption #4: We Don't Need to Be Concerned with Data Quality

Anyone who has worked with data extensively, especially in support of decision making, knows that data quality is important. Data that contains errors beyond a certain threshold is unreliable. For many years organizations have spent a great deal of time and money in their efforts to improve the quality of their data by cleansing it of errors. According to Mayer-Schönberger and Cukier, this is no longer a concern now that we have Big Data.

> *In a world of small data, reducing errors and ensuring high*
> *quality of data was a natural and essential impulse...*
> *However, in many new situations that are cropping up today,*
> *allowing for imprecision—for messiness—may be a positive*
> *feature, not a shortcoming. It is a tradeoff. In return for*
> *relaxing the standards of allowable errors, one can get ahold*
> *of much more data. It isn't just that "more trumps some,"*
> *but that, in fact, sometimes "more trumps better."* [15]

According to them, not only can we stop worrying about messiness in data, we can embrace it as beneficial.

> *In dealing with ever more comprehensive datasets, which*
> *capture not just a small sliver of the phenomenon at hand*
> *but much more or all of it, we no longer need to worry so*
> *much about individual data points biasing the overall*
> *analysis. Rather than aiming to stamp out every bit of*
> *inexactitude at increasingly high cost, we are calculating with*
> *messiness in mind...Though it may seem counterintuitive at*
> *first, treating data as something imperfect and imprecise lets*
> *us make superior forecasts, and thus understand our world*
> *better.* [16]

Hold on. Something is amiss in their reasoning. Although it is true that a particular *amount* of error in a set of data becomes less of a problem if that amount of error holds steady as the total amount of data increases and becomes huge, a particular *rate* of error remains just as much of a problem as the data set grows in size. More data does not trump better data. A sufficient amount of good data has always been the goal.

So what is it that we supposedly get in exchange for our willingness to embrace messiness?

> *In return for living with messiness, we get tremendously*
> *valuable services that would be impossible at their scope and*
> *scale with traditional methods and tools. According to some*
> *estimates only 5 percent of all digital data is 'structured'—*

that is, in a form that fits neatly into a traditional database. Without accepting messiness, the remaining 95 percent of unstructured data, such as web pages and videos, remain dark. By allowing for imprecision, we open a window into an untapped universe of insights. [17]

Mayer-Schönberger and Cukier ignore the fact that data cannot be analyzed until it is structured to some degree. Only then can it produce any of the insights that they celebrate. It doesn't need to reside in a so-called structured database, but it must at a minimum be structured in a virtual sense.

Only those who have never actually worked with data to learn something and then do something about it suffer from the naïve notion that Big Data eliminates or even reduces our concern for data quality.

Assumption #5: We No Longer Need Subject Matter Expertise

I was surprised when Mayer-Schönberger and Cukier, both subject matter experts in their particular realms, added the following claim to their list of errors: "We are seeing the waning of subject-matter experts' influence in many areas." [18]

It is true that the perceived valued of expertise has declined as the Internet has created the impression that Google searches can replace the need for study and experience. Mayer-Schönberger and Cukier argue that subject matter experts will and should be substantially displaced by Big Data because data contains a better understanding of the world than the experts. "Yet expertise is like exactitude: appropriate for a small-data world where one never has enough information, or the right information, and thus has to rely on intuition and experience to guide one's way." [19] Data might contain better, more comprehensive knowledge, but data does not contain understanding. Understanding is formed in the brain of a human. By studying data and the understanding that others have acquired by processing data, and by practicing what they learn, people develop expertise in particular subject areas. Separating subject matter expertise on the one hand from what we can learn from data on the other hand is artificial. All true experts are informed by data. The best experts are well informed by data. Data about things existed long before the digital age. Nothing about data in recent years has changed this.

At one point in their book, Mayer-Schönberger and Cukier quoted Hal Varian, formerly a professor in the computer science department at the University of California, Berkeley and now Google's chief economist: "Data is so widely available and so strategically important that the scarce thing is the knowledge to extract wisdom from it." [20] What they seem to miss is the fact that Varian, in the same interview from which this quotation was derived, talked about the need for subject matter experts such as managers to become better informed by data to do their jobs. People become better subject matter experts when they become better acquainted with pertinent data. These experts will not be displaced by data; they will be enriched by it as they always have been, hopefully to an increasing degree.

> As we've seen, the pioneers in big data often come from fields outside the domain where they make their mark. They are specialists in data analysis, artificial intelligence, mathematics, or statistics, and they apply those skills to specific industries. [21]

No one can perform wonders with data independent of domain expertise. Understanding of data can only be achieved in close collaboration with subject area expertise. Analytical skills do not replace or supplant subject matter expertise, they inform it.

To illustrate how Big Data is displacing the subject matter experts in one industry, Mayer-Schönberger and Cukier wrote the following about the effects of Big Data in journalism: "This is a humbling reminder to the high priests of mainstream media that the public is in aggregate more knowledgeable than they are, and that cufflinked journalists must compete against bloggers in their bathrobes." [22] "Cufflinked journalists"? From where did this characterization of journalists come? Perhaps Cukier, data editor of *The Economist*, has a bone to pick with other journalists who don't understand or respect his work. Whatever the source of this enmity against mainstream media, I don't want to rely on bloggers for my news of the world. While bloggers have useful information to share, unless they develop journalistic skills, they will not replace mainstream journalists. This is definitely one of those cases in which the amount of information—noise in the blogosphere—cannot replace thoughtful and skilled reporting.

Perhaps the strangest twist on this theme is contained in Mayer-Schönberger's and Cukier's belief that, as the skills needed to work with Big Data increase, their value will diminish, for "eventually most value will be in the data itself." [23] The value of skills and expertise will not diminish over time. In fact, it will increase; I hope that appreciation for these skills will increase as well. When programming jobs started being offshored, the value of programming wasn't diminished even though the cost of individual programmers was reduced through competition. No shift in value will occur from skills and expertise to data itself. Data will forever remain untapped, inert, and worthless without the expertise that is required to make sense of it and tie it to existing knowledge.

The notion that more data and new techniques for processing data displace tried and true data-sensemaking methods is especially appealing to those who haven't learned those methods and don't want to. Anderson, Mayer-Schönberger, and Cukier are not skilled data sensemakers. However talented they might be in their own realms, their understanding of data and its use is limited. Their notions about Big Data are naïve, regressive, and downright dangerous. To understand data and its use, we must talk to people who have developed expertise in this work. Generations of such people have worked hard to get us where we are. Let's halt the regression to a less-enlightened age that is embedded in the techno-magical claims of Big Data.

CHAPTER 6 – BIG DATA, BIG BROTHER

Big Data is being used to conceal and justify dangerous misuses of our personal data.

Data can be used in harmful ways. So-called Big Data, in particular, is working in the shadows to do great harm. This often goes unnoticed because of the indiscriminate trust that people tend to place in technologies, as if technologies are benign. Although it is true in one sense that "guns don't kill people, people do," that does not eliminate the need to do what we can to reduce gun violence. The same applies to data and its use. We must create and use technologies ethically.

As I've already shown, there are good reasons to abandon Big Data without even considering its harmful uses. For this reason, and because the potential dangers inherent in Big Data are already well documented, I won't dwell on this particular problem. Instead, I'll briefly describe the concerns that others have already expressed.

My allusion in this chapter's title to Orwell's dystopian nightmare of "Big Brother" suggests that governments are using Big Data to do harm. That is true, but the dangers are not limited to government uses. Many non-governmental organizations that exercise influence over our lives are also using Big Data to do harm.

Weapons of Math Destruction

In her marvelous book, *Weapons of Math Destruction: How Big Data Increases Inequality and Threatens Democracy,* Cathy O'Neil reveals the dangers of algorithms that employ statistics to score people and institutions for various purposes in ways that are unsound, unfair, and yes, destructive. O'Neill identifies several striking examples of these weapons of math destruction (WMDs) in various realms, including those that evaluate teachers, identify potential criminals, screen job applicants and college admission candidates, target people for expensive payday loans, and price loans and insurance variably to take advantage of the people who are most vulnerable.

Following the financial meltdown that was caused in part by WMDs, O'Neill became increasingly concerned that the Big Data movement could lead to harm.

> *More and more, I worried about the separation between technical models and real people, and about the moral repercussions of that separation. In fact, I saw the same pattern emerging that I'd witnessed in finance: a false sense of security was leading to widespread use of imperfect models, self-serving definitions of success, and growing feedback loops. Those who objected were regarded as nostalgic Luddites.*

> *I wondered what the analogue to the credit crisis might be in Big Data. Instead of a bust, I saw a growing dystopia, with inequality rising. The algorithms would make sure that those deemed losers would remain that way. A lucky minority would gain ever more control over the data economy, raking in outrageous fortunes and convincing themselves all the while that they deserved it.* [1]

WMDs are misuses of computers and data.

> *WMDs…tend to favor efficiency. By their very nature they feed on data that can be measured and counted. But fairness is squishy and hard to quantify. It is a concept. And computers, for all of their advances in language and logic, still struggle mightily with concepts…And the concept of fairness utterly escapes them…So fairness isn't calculated into WMDs. And the result is massive, industrial production of unfairness.* [2]

WMDs are sometimes created and used with good intentions, and they are passionately defended, but that doesn't excuse them.

> *Injustice, whether based on greed or prejudice, has been with us forever. And you could argue that WMDs are no worse*

than the human nastiness of the recent past. In many cases,
after all, a loan officer or hiring manager would routinely
exclude entire races, not to mention an entire gender, from
being considered for a mortgage or a job offer. Even the worst
mathematical models, many would argue, aren't nearly that
bad.

But human decision making, while often flawed, has one
chief virtue. It can evolve. As human beings learn and adapt,
we change, and so do our processes. Automated systems, by
contrast, stay stuck in time until engineers dive in to change
them...Big Data processes codify the past. They do not invent
the future. Doing that requires moral imagination, and that's
something only humans can provide. [3]

Growing Concerns

O'Neil isn't alone in her concerns. The list of articles and papers
that have been written to expose the dangers lurking in Big Data is
long and growing. Here's an excerpt from an article, written by
Adam Frank for National Public Radio (NPR):

The central premise of Big Data is that all the digital
breadcrumbs we leave behind as we go about our everyday
lives create a trail of behavior that can be followed, captured,
stored and "mined" en masse, providing the miners with
fundamental insights into both our personal and collective
behavior.

The initial "ick" factor from Big Data is the loss of privacy, as
pretty much every aspect of your life (location records via
mobile phones, purchases via credit cards, interests via
web-surfing behavior) has been recorded—and, possibly,
shared—by some entity somewhere. Big Data moves from
"ick" to potentially harmful when all of those breadcrumbs
are thrown in a machine for processing.

This is the "data-mining" part of Big Data and it happens

when algorithms are used to search for statistical correlations
between one kind of behavior and another. This is where
things can get really tricky and really scary. [4]

Many technology vendors are already earning huge revenues by
invading our privacy and misappropriating our data. They argue
that the data isn't ours, it's theirs, by virtue of the fact that we enter
it into their systems or it is generated when we use their systems. It
shouldn't surprise us that these same vendors push us to accept the
sacrifice of our privacy as inevitable and even beneficial. Back in
1999, Sun Microsystems CEO Scott McNealy proclaimed, "You have
zero privacy anyway...Get over it." [5] More recently, Mark Zuckerberg
of Facebook similarly declared that "the age of privacy is over." [6]
Concerned about self-serving declarations such as these, Neil M.
Richards and Jonathan H. King issued the following warning:

> *Such techno-centric worldviews carry an implied undertone*
> *of technology infallibility. We must yield our expectations of*
> *privacy, they suggest, to make way for the inevitable, and get*
> *out of the way of technological innovation.*
>
> *Yet Edward Snowden and Glenn Greenwald's revelations*
> *about the scale of surveillance by the National Security*
> *Agency have prompted a global debate about surveillance*
> *and privacy that continues months later. Why is this*
> *happening if privacy is dead? We would like to suggest, to the*
> *contrary, that privacy is not dead. Privacy is very much alive,*
> *though it, like other social norms, is in a state of flux.* [7]

Our loss of privacy is not inevitable. If technocrats who benefit
from its loss have their way, however, we will surrender our privacy
without notice and without choice. We can and must resist.
Richards and King believe that we can and should curtail the loss of
privacy:

> *We need to ensure that we think ethically about big data and*
> *other new information technologies. These technologies are*
> *not "natural" and foreordained; they are the product of*
> *human choices and they will affect human values. We need*

to be sure that these human technologies shape the kind of
society we want to have, for these technologies will shape the
societies we will live in and the humans we will become. [8]

Similarly, Ian Kerr and Jessica Earle have drawn attention to Big
Data's penchant for prediction as an insidious threat.

Contrary to the received view, our central concern about big
data is not about the data. It is about big data's power to
enable a dangerous new philosophy of preemption…Our
concern is that big data's promise of increased efficiency,
reliability, utility, profit, and pleasure might be seen as the
justification for a fundamental jurisprudential shift from our
current ex post facto system of penalties and punishments to
ex ante preventative measures that are increasingly being
adopted across various sectors of society. It is our contention
that big data's predictive benefits belie an important insight
historically represented in the presumption of innocence and
associated privacy and due process values—namely, that
there is wisdom in setting boundaries around the kinds of
assumptions that can and cannot be made about people.

…

With this insight, an important concern arises. Big data's
escalating interest in and successful use of preemptive
predictions as a means of avoiding risk becomes a catalyst for
various new forms of social preemption. More and more,
governments, corporations, and individuals will use big data
to preempt or forestall activities perceived to generate social
risk. Often, this will be done with little or no transparency or
accountability. Some loan companies, for example, are
beginning to use algorithms to determine interest rates for
clients with little to no credit history, and to decide who is at
high risk for default. Thousands of indicators are analyzed,
ranging from the presence of financially secure friends on
Facebook to time spent on websites and apps installed on
various data devices. Governments, in the meantime, are

using this technique in a variety of fields in order to deter-
mine the distribution of scarce resources such as social
workers for at-risk youth or entitlement to Medicaid, food
stamps, and welfare compensation. [9]

Behind the benign mask of Big Data resides a long list of malicious practices that have come to light. Here are a few:

- Algorithms that evaluate people, resulting in the denial of
  opportunities (jobs, loans, etc.)
- Algorithms that stack the deck against those who are most
  vulnerable (over-priced loans, over-priced insurance, etc.)
- Algorithms that identify people as potential bad actors who
  have committed no bad actions (possible terrorists on no-fly
  lists, individuals targeted as likely criminals, etc.)
- Algorithms that invade our privacy by using personal
  information against our interests (racial profiling, financial
  profiling, unwarranted marketing, etc.)
- Algorithms that invade our privacy by tracking what we do
  (unauthorized GPS tracking of our location; surveillance of
  our communications, purchases, or Internet searches, etc.)
- Algorithms that deliver varying messages to different groups
  of people for manipulative purposes based on information
  gleaned from social media or Internet searches (Facebook ads
  purchased by political groups that target specific groups of
  people based on their social media content, Internet searches
  with false information that is designed to trigger the fears of
  specific groups of people, marketing messages targeting people
  who are demographically susceptible to specific forms of
  deceit, etc.)

Sadly, even if Big Data is recognized as the illusion that it is and
abandoned, unethical uses of data will not necessarily end. Some
people and organizations will always attempt to use data for their
own self-serving and sometimes malicious ends. To guard against

abuses, we must create and enforce laws that match in sophistication the clever ways that are emerging to misappropriate data.

In his book *Ethics of Big Data*, Kord Davis warns that "the potential for harm due to unintended consequences can quickly outweigh the value the big-data innovation is intended to provide." [10] I agree. Exposing Big Data as a charade won't solve these problems, but it will certainly get us closer.

EPILOGUE – BIG DATA, BIG DARE

We must abandon Big Data to begin using data in effective ways.

If you understand and accept the case that I've made in this book, I dare you to do something about it. When enough of us do, Big Data will fade from the scene. If this happens, where will it leave us? We'll be left with data, which is where we've always been. This is not a bad place to be. Data can provide enormous benefits when it is understood and used for good. The sooner we recognize that data is data is data, that its value can only be tapped by first understanding it, and that understanding primarily requires human skills, the sooner we can put data to use for good. Almost everything that is worthwhile results from hard work. It's time that we got down to it.

Data, in and of itself, is of no value. Data is only valuable as a source of information that leads to understanding. The goal is understanding, not amassing data. Better yet, the goal is better decisions and actions that are based on understanding. The vision that has been propagated by Big Data, with its emphasis on Big as inherently useful and Data as valuable in and of itself, is fundamentally flawed. A shift in emphasis is needed to fuel meaningful progress: from "Big" to "Thorough and Clear" and from "Data" to "Understanding." I suffer from no illusions that "Thorough and Clear Understanding" will ever inspire public attention in the way "Big Data" has, but real progress isn't measured in Web views and clicks or in technology vendor revenues. Real progress is measured by each wise decision that makes our world a little better.

There are things in this world that are worth fighting for. Technological illusions are not on this list. By focusing on the Big Data illusion, we've lost our way. It's time to remember what matters and abandon all that prevents us from achieving and maintaining it. Technologies, in and of themselves, don't matter. The best of our technologies can help us achieve and maintain what matters. The best technologies don't need to be promoted by misinformation and false promises. The best technologies fit our hands like gloves and extend our reach with precise and steady aim, always under the control of skilled and wise humans.

There's a complicated world out there, filled with injustice and suffering. Data won't save us from the problems of that world. Information is valuable only when we use it wisely to do something worthwhile. We're the protagonists in this story; information is only a resource.

I recently had breakfast with a fellow who works as a computer security expert. He helps organizations identify, track, and prevent cybercrimes. What inspires him to get up each morning? He has a chance to catch the "bad guys." He uses his skills, honed through years of experience, to examine information in an effort to identify those doing harm and to stop them. He makes this happen, not data.

The value of information should be measured in terms of useful outcomes. Did your understanding increase? If so, did that understanding relate to things that matter? If so, did that understanding produce better decisions and actions? Only when you can answer "Yes" to each of these questions was the information—and the technology that helped you understand it—worthwhile.

The Slow Data Movement

In 1986, Carlo Petrini founded the "Slow Food Movement." This movement began as resistance to the opening of a McDonald's fast-food restaurant near the Spanish Steps in Rome. I've seen this affront to the old city and felt the disgust that must have emboldened Petrini to start an international movement. Slow food was introduced as an alternative to fast food. The movement is based on the belief that much of the beauty and wholesomeness of food requires that we take time with it: time in producing it, time in preparing it, time in savoring it. The Slow Food Movement is one of a broader collection of Slow Movements that focus on many aspects of life.

It is not surprising that in our fast-paced world we need to be reminded to slow down and embrace life with greater awareness and appreciation, lest we forget who we are and what makes life worth living. I believe that it is time to extend the Slow Movement to the realm of data. Too much is being missed in the rush. The entire point of collecting data—using information to better under-stand our world and then make well-informed decisions based on that understanding—has been forgotten and is certainly not being achieved in our manic rush to throw more technology at a problem that can only be solved by more carefully using our brains.

Big Data is often defined in terms of the 3Vs: volume, velocity, and variety. When Doug Laney originally proposed the 3Vs, they were already old news. I remember reading Laney's paper at the time and thinking that he did a good job of characterizing signifi-cant aspects of data that had been true since the advent of the computer. In contrast to the 3Vs, I'd like to propose the correcting influence of the 3Ss: Small, Slow, and Sure.

Small

As data increases in volume, we should keep in mind that only a relatively small amount of it is useful. Data consists of much noise and only a little signal. We must separate the signals from the noise, which we'll never get around to doing if we spend all of our time implementing technologies for data generation and collection without ever learning how to find and understand what's actually meaningful and useful.

Slow

We're in love with speed. Like many people, I love to drive fast. It's a rush. Much of what I value in life, however, requires time. This is especially true of data sensemaking and decision making. Some of my favorite words were spoken by Lao Tzu, the founder of Taoism: "Muddy water, let stand, becomes clear." These words have come to mind and thus to the rescue many times in my life. The book *Wait:*

The Art and Science of Delay by Frank Partnoy, roots the benefits of waiting, pausing, and taking a bit more time, in science. In the introduction Partnoy says:

> *The essence of my case is this: given the fast pace of modern life, most of us tend to react too quickly. We don't, or can't, take enough time to think about the increasingly complex timing challenges we face. Technology surrounds us, speeding us up. We feel its crush every day, both at work and at home. Yet the best time managers are comfortable pausing for as long as necessary before they act, even in the face of the most pressing decisions. Some seem to slow down time. For good decision-makers, time is more flexible than a metronome or atomic clock...As we will see over and over, in most situations we should take more time than we do.* [1]

Although some decisions in life are best made instantly, based on intuition, this is only true if your intuitions were built on a great deal of relevant experience and the matter at hand does not lend itself to deliberation. These are the types of decisions that Malcolm Gladwell wrote about in *Blink*. Most non-routine decisions, however, especially those that change the course of our lives, benefit from conscious, deliberate, reflective, analytical reasoning—what psychologists such as Daniel Kahneman call "System 2 Thinking." In fact, Kahneman refers to the two modes of reasoning I describe above as "thinking fast" and "thinking slow."

No matter how rapidly data is generated and transmitted, the act of data sensemaking, which must precede data's use, is necessarily a slow process. We must take time to understand information and act upon it wisely. Speed will, in most cases, lead to mistakes.

Sure

Even though we can collect data about everything imaginable, variety is not always a boon. More choices are only helpful if we need them, and we have the time and means to consider them. Otherwise, they do nothing but complicate our already complicated lives.

In an effort to remain sane, I spend a fair amount of time limiting my choices. For instance, I don't participate in *Twitter*, *Facebook*, or even *LinkedIn* because I already face enough interaction with people. By restricting myself mostly to email correspondence and direct face-to-face conversations, I maintain the level of human interaction that works for me. I'm not suggesting that these social media services are bad; they just don't suit me. The next time that you're in a grocery store browsing the toothpaste section, ask yourself if the variety of products arranged in daunting rows is useful. Wouldn't just a few good choices make life better?

Our lives and our world are rich in variety. This is good. Data is a collection of facts about our rich varied life and world. Only a subset of those facts will be useful to us. Just because we can collect data about something doesn't mean we should. In fact, given all the data that we've already collected, wouldn't it make sense to spend more time making use of it rather than getting wrapped up in the acquisition of more? When you recognize an opportunity to do something useful with data, that's when it becomes sure. By "sure," I'm not suggested that data is ever utterly certain but that it is reliable. As people and organizations of limited resources, shouldn't we spend our time identifying what's useful and then actually using it?

The Path to a Solution

Data is growing in *volume*, as it always has, but only a *small* amount of it is useful. Data is being generated and transmitted at an increasing *velocity*, but the race is not necessarily for the swift; *slow* and steady will win the information race if understanding is our goal. Data is branching out in ever-greater *variety*, but only a few of these new choices are *sure*. *Small*, *slow*, and *sure* should be our focus if we want to use data effectively to create a better world. I doubt that the 3Ss that I've proposed will ever become the rallying cry of a mighty movement, but those who heed them will likely become the true heroes of an Information Age worthy of the name. When the dust settles, we'll see that the people who solved the problems of our age took the time to analyze a limited collection of the right data.

The path that I'm proposing is challenging. The primary challenge is not learning the skills that are needed to mine value from data even though this does indeed involve hard work. The real challenge is the change in perception and commitment that our organizations must effect to begin the work. To launch the journey, organizations must come to grips with each of the following precepts:

1. Useful information can be derived from data.
2. Only relevant data of good quality is useful.
3. Information is only useful if it is understood.
4. The steps that lead to understanding—what I call data sensemaking—require skills that must be learned.
5. The development of data-sensemaking skills involves a great deal of study and practice.
6. Study and practice take time—lots of time.
7. Technologies are needed to augment human data-sensemaking abilities.
8. Only well-designed technologies are worth the investment of time and money.
9. Skilled data sensemakers combine general analytical skills with specific domain knowledge; one without the other is not enough.

Data sensemaking requires a significant investment in the development of human skills. Organizations can hire people with these skills, but that is unlikely to suffice. Much of the talent that's needed must be grown and cultivated within the organization. Education is the key.

It isn't easy to get an organization to accept these facts, but they are true, and only the truth will free us to harvest the bounty that resides in data. There are no quick, easy, magical solutions. There never were, and there never will be. It's time to reject the magical thinking that IT vendors have been encouraging us to embrace at great price. It's time to demonstrate some true intelligence.

Choose the road less travelled. I dare you.

REFERENCES

Chapter 1

1. Cox, Michael and David Ellsworth. 1997. "Application-controlled demand paging for out-of-core visualization." *VIS '97 Proceedings of the 8th conference on Visualization.*
2. Cukier, Kenneth. February 25, 2010. "Data, data everywhere." *The Economist.* <http://www.economist.com/node/15557443>
3. Mayer-Schönberger, Viktor and Kenneth Cukier. 2013. *Big Data: A Revolution That Will Transform How We Live, Work, and Think.* New York, NY: Houghton Mifflin Harcourt. p. 6.
4. Ibid. p. 2.
5. Ibid. pp. 11-12.
6. Ibid. p. 190.
7. Ibid. pp. 6-7.
8. Ibid. p. 7.
9. Ibid. p. 100.
10. "What is Big Data?" SAS Institute, Inc. <https://www.sas.com/en_us/insights/big-data/what-is-big-data.html>
11. Beal, Vangie. "Big Data." *Webopedia.* <https://www.webopedia.com/TERM/B/big_data.html>
12. Varian, Hal (Chief Economist, Google). *
13. Granville, Vincent (Co-Founder, Data Science Central). *
14. Foreman, John (Chief Data Scientist, MailChimp). *
15. White, John Myles. *
16. Greiner, Annette (Lecturer, University of California, Berkeley School of Information). *
17. Schwartz, Josh (Chief Data Scientist, Chartbeat). *
18. Hardy, Quentin (Deputy Tech Editor, *The New York Times*). *
19. "What is Big Data?" Gartner, Inc. <https://www.gartner.com/it-glossary/big-data>
20. Ashlock, Philip (Chief Architect, Data.gov). *
21. "Big Data." *Wikipedia, the Free Encyclopedia.* Wikimedia Foundation. <https://en.wikipedia.org/wiki/Big_data>
22. Upadhyay, Shashi (CEO and Founder, Lattice Engines). *

23. Bryant, Reid (Data Scientist, Brooks Bell). *
24. Cavaretta, Mike (Data Scientist and Manager, Ford Motor Company). *
25. Swanstrom, Ryan (Data Science Blogger, "Data Science 101" blog). *
26. Dresner, Howard. 1989.

---

* Note: All of the references marked with an asterisk are quotes that originally appeared in the following article:

Dutcher, Jennifer. September 3, 2014. "What is Big Data?" University of California, Berkeley School of Information. <https://datascience.berkeley.edu/what-is-big-data/>

Chapter 2

1. Jones, Martyn. December 20, 2014. "Big Data is Dead." *Good Strategy.* <https://goodstrat.com/2014/12/20/big-data-is-dead/>
2. Ariely, Dan. January 6, 2013. "Big data is like teenage sex..." *Facebook.* <https://www.facebook.com/dan.ariely/posts/904383595868?imm_mid=0a9701&cmp=em-strata-newsletters-strata-olc-20130529-elist>
3. Victoroff, Slater. September 10, 2015. "Big Data Doesn't Exist." *Crunch Network.* <https://techcrunch.com/2015/09/10/big-data-doesnt-exist/>
4. Mayer-Schönberger, Viktor and Kenneth Cukier. 2013. *Big Data: A Revolution That Will Transform How We Live, Work, and Think.* New York, NY: Houghton Mifflin Harcourt. p. 6.
5. Ibid. p. 151.
6. Ibid. p. 179.
7. Ibid. p. 190.

Chapter 3

1. *The Bible*. 1978. New International Version. Mark 2:22.
2. Davenport, Thomas. 2014. *Big Data at Work*. Boston, MA: Harvard Business School Publishing Corporation. p. 7.
3. Ibid. p. 77.
4. Ibid. p. 1.
5. Ibid. p. 118.
6. Kolb, Jason and Jeremy Kolb. 2013. *The Big Data Revolution*. Applied Data Labs. p. 10.
7. Ibid. p. 11.
8. Ibid. p. 19.
9. Ibid. p. 74.
10. Ibid. p. 109.
11. Ibid. p. 110.
12. Ibid. p. 123.
13. Ibid. p. 127.
14. Manyika, James, et. al. May 2011. "Big data: The next frontier for innovation, competition, and productivity." McKinsey Global Institute. <https://www.mckinsey.com/business-functions/digital-mckinsey/our-insights/big-data-the-next-frontier-for-innovation>
15. Marr, Bernard. December 16, 2014. "The Big Data Economy: Here's What You Must Know." *LinkedIn*. <https://www.linkedin.com/pulse/big-data-economy-heres-what-you-bernard-marr>
16. Mayer-Schönberger, Viktor and Kenneth Cukier. 2013. *Big Data: A Revolution That Will Transform How We Live, Work, and Think*. New York, NY: Houghton Mifflin Harcourt. p. 60.
17. Ibid. p. 15.
18. Ibid. p. 103.
19. Ibid. p. 110.
20. Ibid. p. 146.

Chapter 4

1. Jones, Martyn. December 20, 2014. "Big Data is Dead." *Good Strategy.* <https://goodstrat.com/2014/12/20/big-data-is-dead/>
2. Taleb, Nassim N. February 8, 2013. " Beware the Big Errors of Big Data." *Wired.* <https://www.wired.com/2013/02/big-data-means-big-errors-people/>
3. Millay, Edna St. Vincent. 1939. "Huntsman, What Quarry?"

Chapter 5

1. Ginsberg, Jeremy, et al. February 19, 2009. "Detecting influenza epidemics using search engine query data." *Nature* Volume 457. pp. 1,012-1,014.
2. Spiegelhalter, David. Quoted by Tim Harford. March 28, 2014. "Big data: are we making a big mistake?" *The Financial Times.* <https://www.ft.com/content/21a6e7d8-b479-11e3-a09a-00144feabdc0>
3. Harford, Tim. March 28, 2014. "Big data: are we making a big mistake?" *The Financial Times.* <https://www.ft.com/content/21a6e7d8-b479-11e3-a09a-00144feabdc0>
4. Mayer-Schönberger, Viktor and Kenneth Cukier. 2013. *Big Data: A Revolution That Will Transform How We Live, Work, and Think.* New York, NY: Houghton Mifflin Harcourt. p. 18.
5. Ibid. p. 66.
6. Anderson, Chris. June 23, 2008. "The End of Theory: The Data Deluge Makes the Scientific Method Obsolete." *Wired Magazine.* <https://www.wired.com/2008/06/pb-theory/>
7. Ibid.
8. Harford, Tim. March 28, 2014. "Big data: are we making a big mistake?" *The Financial Times.* <https://www.ft.com/content/21a6e7d8-b479-11e3-a09a-00144feabdc0>
9. Malak, Michael. October 27, 2014. "Wired's 'End of Theory' Six Years Later." Data Science Association blog. <http://www.datascienceassn.org/content/wireds-end-theory-six-years-later>

10. Ibid.
11. Anderson, Chris. June 23, 2008. "The End of Theory: The Data Deluge Makes the Scientific Method Obsolete." *Wired Magazine*. <https://www.wired.com/2008/06/pb-theory/>
12. Bridle, James. November 1, 2006. "What's wrong with big data?" *New Humanist*. <https://newhumanist.org.uk/articles/5104/whats-wrong-with-big-data>
13. Box, G. E. P. May 1979. "Robustness in the Strategy of Scientific Model Building." University of Wisconsin-Madison Mathematics Research Center.
14. Harford, Tim. March 28, 2014. "Big data: are we making a big mistake?" *The Financial Times*. <https://www.ft.com/content/21a6e7d8-b479-11e3-a09a-00144feabdc0>
15. Mayer-Schönberger, Viktor and Kenneth Cukier. 2013. *Big Data: A Revolution That Will Transform How We Live, Work, and Think*. New York, NY: Houghton Mifflin Harcourt. pp. 32-33.
16. Ibid. pp. 40-41.
17. Ibid. p. 47.
18. Ibid. p. 141.
19. Ibid. p. 142.
20. Ibid. p. 125.
21. Ibid. p. 142.
22. Ibid. p. 103.
23. Ibid. p. 134.

Chapter 6

1. O'Neil, Cathy. 2016. *Weapons of Math Destruction*. New York, NY: Crown. p. 48.
2. Ibid. p. 95.
3. Ibid. pp. 203-204.
4. Frank, Adam. June 11, 2013. "A Brave New World: Big Data's Big Dangers." NPR. <http://www.npr.org/sections/13.7/2013/06/10/190516689/a-brave-new-world-big-datas-big-dangers>

5. McNealy, Scott. Quoted by Polly Sprenger. January 26, 1999. "Sun on Privacy: 'Get over it'" *Wired Magazine.* <https://www.wired.com/1999/01/sun-on-privacy-get-over-it/>
6. Zuckerberg, Mark. Quoted by Marshall Kirkpatrick. January 9, 2010. "Facebook's Zuckerberg Says The Age of Privacy is Over." ReadWrite. <https://readwrite.com/2010/01/09/facebooks_zuckerberg_says_the_age_of_privacy_is_ov/>
7. Richards, Neil M. and Jonathan H. King. May 19, 2014. "Big Data Ethics." *Wake Forest Law Review*, volume 49. pp. 409-410.
8. Ibid. p. 426.
9. Kerr, Ian and Jessica Earle. September 3, 2013. "Prediction, Preemption, Presumption: How Big Data Threatens Big Picture Privacy." *66 Stanford Law Review Online 65.* <https://www.stanfordlawreview.org/online/privacy-and-big-data-prediction-preemption-presumption/>
10. David, Kord. September 2012. *Ethics of Big Data: Balancing Risk and Innovation.* Sebastopol, CA: O'Reilly Media. p. 5.

Epilogue

1. Partnoy, Frank. June 26, 2012. *Wait: The Art and Science of Delay.* New York, NY: PublicAffairs. p. xi-xii.

INDEX